BTRIPP BOOKS

BOOK REVIEWS FROM

2007

BY BRENDAN TRIPP

*These reviews originally appeared on the
"BTRIPP'S BOOKS" book review blog:
http://btripp-books.livejournal.com/*

Copyright © 2016 by Brendan Tripp

ISBN 978-1-57353-407-9

An Eschaton Book

*Front cover photo courtesy Kenn W. Kiser via morguefile.com.
Back cover photo courtesy Sebastian Santana via morguefile.com.*

PREFACE

From 1993 through 2004, I ran the *first* manifestation of Eschaton Books (now in its third revival). Initially started as a vehicle to publish my poetry, it soon became evident that the market for poetry is vanishingly small, and in 1994 we "pivoted" into being a metaphysical press.

In this time, I was largely a one-man shop, doing everything from editorial to shipping, which was a huge time commitment, and I typically worked 14 hour days, 7 days a week to keep things moving. I bring up all this here because, despite having been a life-long avid reader, during this period I had precious little time for reading, and what reading I *did* get done was largely reviewing book submissions. However, I never stopped *buying* books, which began to stack up in prodigious "to be read" piles.

When Eschaton went out of business in 2004 (in a not unusual denouement for a small press – we had a distributor who ended up never paying us, while selling through all our stock), I found myself with a lot of reading to catch up on, and a need to keep my writing chops sharp. So, I began to pen little reviews of what I was reading, and post those on the web.

As the years went by, this became "a thing" that I was doing, and, for a while, I was targeting a fairly aggressive goal of getting at least 72 non-fiction books read per year. By 2015, this had resulted in my having read and reviewed 700 books over that 12-year span.

In recent years (since the upswing in print-on-demand publishing), I have had numerous acquaintances suggest that I put out my reviews as books. I was, at first, rather hesitant on the concept (as, after all, the material was free to read on the web), but I eventually figured that if various people thought it was a good idea, I might as well give it a shot.

While I could have started at the beginning, with the reviews from 2004, I decided that those were less representative of the whole, so opted to begin with the most recent ones.

This is the ninth of these collections, and definitely shows its age in spots, not only in the context it was written (both reflecting what was happening in my life and in the world), but in the length of reviews, which, generally speaking, have gotten shorter the further back we go. Please pardon the extensive "white space" that this has produced among these 79 reviews!

There were a couple of people who were interested in helping sell these who were encouraging me to go to a "flat rate" per volume, which I was initially resistant to. While the print-on-demand tech is wonderful, the costs are fairly high per copy, and there had to be "enough meat on the bone" to make it into the wider wholesale markets (such as when a bookstore orders in a copy), so I had to pick a cover price that would cover that, or not be able to sell through those channels.

After messing around with the numbers, I picked the rather odd $15.97 as the price ... it's "sort of" numerologically derived, being both a prime number, and a part of the famed Fibonacci sequence ... which is both less than what most of the books had been priced (at the quarter-per-review rate I'd first come up with), and enough for even the longer page-count volumes to get into "extended distribution".

As noted in previous intros, I do not write classic reviews, but more a telling of my personal interaction with a particular book. This means that I talk about where and how I got the book, how it relates to other things I've read, what sort of reactions it triggered in me (and why), and how one can get a copy if it sounds appealing. I recently read a biography of Hunter S. Thompson, and noted some similarity in my reviewing style to how his "journalistic style" was being described ... but I'm not sure I'm ready to try to assume the mantle of "Gonzo". Needless to say, if the reader is devoted to "standard" book reviewing styles, this might be an irritation ... however, it does make these reviews somewhat idiosyncratic to me, resulting in a collection that is something of a "my encounters with books" sort of deal, which will, hopefully, be of interest to many readers.

- Brendan Tripp

CONTENTS

v - Preface

vii - Contents

1 - Monday, January 1, 2007

A very good book ...
Bias: A CBS Insider Exposes How the Media Distort the News
by Bernard Goldberg

3 - Tuesday, January 16, 2007

Back to the books ...
The Equinox, Volume III, Number 10
by Aleister Crowley / Hymenaeus Beta X°

4 - Wednesday, January 17, 2007

Back-to-back reviews, eh?
Shabono: A Visit to a Remote and Magical World in the South American Rain Forest
by Florinda Donner

6 - Saturday, January 20, 2007

Better late than never, I guess ...
The Wheel of Time: The Kalachakra in Context
by Geshe Lhundub Sopa

8 - Wednesday, January 24, 2007

Can't say much about this one ...
Kalacakra Tantra
by Geshe Ngawang Dhargyey

9 - Monday, January 29, 2007

That was a long read ...
Black Holes and Time Warps: Einstein's Outrageous Legacy
by Kip Thorne

11 - Tuesday, February 13, 2007

One last (I think) on the Kalachakra ...
The Practice of Kalachakra
by Glenn H. Mullin

13 - Saturday, February 17, 2007

Dalai Lama ...
**Freedom In Exile:
the Autobiography of the Dalai Lama**
by His Holiness the Dalai Lama

15 - Saturday, February 17, 2007

More Tibet ...
Tibet: The Sacred Realm - Photographs 1880-1950
by Lobsang P. Lhalungpa

17 - Sunday, February 25, 2007

I should have read the title ...
**Mountains of the Middle Kingdom:
Exploring the High Peaks of China and Tibet**
by Galen Rowell

19 - Thursday, March 1, 2007

A long read ...
Wisdom and Compassion: The Sacred Art of Tibet
by Marylin M. Rhie & Robert A. F. Thurman

20 - Thursday, March 8, 2007

This started out well ...
Healing and the Mind
by Bill Moyers

22 - Saturday, March 10, 2007

Finally read this one ...
**The Monuments of Mars:
a City On the Edge Of Forever**
by Richard C. Hoagland

24 - Sunday, March 11, 2007

Not something that I just picked up ...
Might is Right: The Survival of the Fittest
by Ragnar Redbeard

26 - Wednesday, March 14, 2007

An odd one ...
**The Andean Codex: Adventures and Initiations
Among the Peruvian Shamans**
by J.E. Williams

28 - Thursday, March 15, 2007

Not what you'd expect ...
The Wheel of Time: The Shamans of Ancient Mexico, Their Thoughts About Life, Death and the Universe
by Carlos Castaneda

30 - Thursday, March 22, 2007

Verrrrrry Interrrresting ...
The Active Side of Infinity
by Carlos Castaneda

32 - Sunday, March 25, 2007

What a shame ...
Magical Passes: The Practical Wisdom of the Shamans of Ancient Mexico
by Carlos Castaneda

35 - Friday, April 6, 2007

If you want a Shamanic book ...
Mending The Past And Healing The Future with Soul Retrieval
by Alberto Villoldo

37 - Sunday, April 8, 2007

(sigh)
Hypnosis: How to Put a Smile on Your Face and Money in Your Pocket
by Shelley Stockwell

39 - Monday, April 16, 2007

A very worthwhile read ...
The Demon-Haunted World: Science as a Candle in the Dark
by Carl Sagan

41 - Thursday, April 19, 2007

A really good book ...
Moral Minority: Our Skeptical Founding Fathers
by Brooke Allen

43 - Friday, April 27, 2007

Clap your hands if you believe ...
The Secret
by Rhonda Byrne

45 - Tuesday, May 1, 2007

Another decent one ...
**The Four Agreements:
A Practical Guide to Personal Freedom,
A Toltec Wisdom Book**
by don Miguel Ruiz

47 - Friday, May 4, 2007

How odd ...
Creating Money: Keys to Abundance
by Sanaya Roman & Duane Packer

49 - Sunday, May 13, 2007

Maybe I just don't "get it" ...
The Power of Now: A Guide to Spiritual Enlightenment
by Eckhart Tolle

51 - Sunday, May 20, 2007

A mixed bag ...
Spirit & Reason: The Vine Deloria, Jr. Reader
by Vine Deloria, Jr.

52 - Thursday, May 24, 2007

another "attraction" approach ...
**The Power of Intention:
Learning to Co-create Your World Your Way**
by Dr. Wayne W. Dyer

54 - Thursday, May 24, 2007

Blew through this one ...
**Fearless Living:
Live without Excuses and Love without Regret**
by Rhonda Britten

56 - Friday, June 1, 2007

Almost didn't add this one ...
Careers for New Agers & Other Cosmic Types
by Blythe Camenson

57 - Monday, June 11, 2007

Well, here's the last of these ...
**The Law of Attraction:
The Basics of the Teachings of Abraham**
by Esther & Jerry Hicks

59 - Tuesday, June 12, 2007

That's more like it ...
Letters to a Young Contrarian
by Christopher Hitchens

61 - Tuesday, June 19, 2007

How odd ...
The Selfish Gene
by Richard Dawkins

63 - Sunday, June 24, 2007

A good one ...
The Mind's Sky:
Human Intelligence in a Cosmic Context
by Timothy Ferris

65 - Wednesday, June 27, 2007

Oh, and this ...
Libertarianism In One Lesson
by David Bergland

67 - Saturday, July 7, 2007

Long time ...
Art & Physics:
Parallel Visions in Space, Time, and Light
by Leonard Shlain

69 - Sunday, July 8, 2007

another ...
The 21 Indispensable Qualities of a Leader:
Becoming the Person Others Will Want to Follow
by John C. Maxwell

70 - Monday, July 9, 2007

Settle down!
Who's Looking Out for You?
by Bill O'Reilly

72 - Monday, July 9, 2007

Hoooo-boy ...
Mayan Vision Quest:
Mystical Initiation in Mesoamerica
by Cynthia MacAdams, Hunbartz Men & Charles Bensinger

74 - Thursday, July 19, 2007

you were wondering, weren't you?
Sacred Journeys:
An Illustrated Guide to Pilgrimages Around the World
by Jennifer Westwood

75 - Monday, July 23, 2007

A very good over-view ...
Gurdjieff: An Introduction to His Life and Ideas
by John Shirley

77 - Wednesday, July 25, 2007

Another good one ...
The Jesus Dynasty: The Hidden History of Jesus,
His Royal Family, and the Birth of Christianity
by James D. Tabor

79 - Friday, August 3, 2007

How ironic ...
Real Success Without a Real Job:
There Is No Life Like It!
by Ernie Zelinski

81 - Saturday, Saturday, August 11, 2007

Big Math ... Weird Science ...
The Cosmic Landscape:
String Theory and the Illusion of Intelligent Design
by Leonard Susskind

83 - Sunday, August 12, 2007

Been meaning to read this one for a while ...
The Englishman's Handbook
by Idries Shah

85 - Monday, August 13, 2007

I was hoping this would help!
The 100 Simple Secrets of Happy People:
What Scientists Have Learned and How You Can Use It
by David Niven, Ph.D.

86 - Wednesday, August 29, 2007

Arrgh ... so behind on these!
A Devil's Chaplain:
Reflections on Hope, Lies, Science, and Love
by Richard Dawkins

88 - Thursday, August 30, 2007

And now to piss off the other half of my readers ...
**Useful Idiots: How Liberals Got It Wrong
in the Cold War and Still Blame America First**
by Mona Charen

90 - Friday, August 31, 2007

An odd one ...
**Mind Sights: Original Visual Illusions, Ambiguities,
and Other Anomalies, With a Commentary
on the Play of Mind in Perception and Art**
by Roger N. Shepard

92 - Sunday, September 9, 2007

A good read ...
**Parenting Beyond Belief:
On Raising Ethical, Caring Kids Without Religion**
by Dale McGowan

94 - Monday, September 10, 2007

More science ...
The Whole Shebang: A State-of-the-Universe(s) Report
by Timothy Ferris

96 - Tuesday, September 11, 2007

Hmmmmm ...
Thoreau: A Book of Quotations
by Henry David Thoreau

98 - Thursday, September 13, 2007

Poetry ... not mine
The Ballad of Reading Gaol and Other Poems
by Oscar Wilde

100 - Sunday, September 16, 2007

Wow ...
Great Speeches by Native Americans
by Bob Blaisdell, Ed.

102 - Thursday, September 20, 2007

"Nietzsche, Nietzsche, Nietzsche!"
The Genealogy of Morals
by Friedrich Nietzsche

104 - Monday, September 24, 2007

As if this needs an introduction ...
Beowulf
by R. K. Gordon, Trans.

106 - Wednesday, September 26, 2007

Lots of pictures ...
Chicago Then And Now
by Elizabeth McNulty

107 - Sunday, September 30, 2007

Spoiler Alert!
The Nibelungenlied
by D.G. Mowatt, Trans.

109 - Sunday, September 30, 2007

Ah, one more for this month ...
The Constitution of the United States with the Declaration of Independence and the Articles of Confederation
by R.B. Bernstein, Intro.

111 - Sunday, October 7, 2007

Fantastic little book!
Letter to a Christian Nation
by Sam Harris

114 - Saturday, October 13, 2007

Hot Stuff ...
**McIlhenny's Gold:
How a Louisiana Family Built the Tabasco Empire**
by Jeffrey Rothfeder

116 - Sunday, October 14, 2007

Important stuff ...
Common Sense, The Rights of Man and Other Essential Writings of Thomas Paine
by Thomas Paine

119 - Wednesday, October 17, 2007

Oh, what fun ...
If Democrats Had Any Brains, They'd Be Republicans
by Ann Coulter

121 - Sunday, October 21, 2007

An odd one ...
From Clocks to Chaos: The Rhythms of Life
by Leon Glass & Michael C. Mackey

123 - Sunday, October 28, 2007

Seven and Mountains and Bears ... OH MY!
Dawn Behind the Dawn:
A Search for the Earthly Paradise
by Geoffrey Ashe

125 - Sunday, November 4, 2007

An excellent Shamanic book ...
The Four Insights:
Wisdom, Power, and Grace of the Earthkeepers
by Alberto Villoldo

128 - Friday, November 9, 2007

Another book that EVERYBODY should read ...
The End of Faith:
Religion, Terror, and the Future of Reason
by Sam Harris

130 - Saturday, November 10, 2007

An "interesting" book ...
The Ape That Spoke:
Language and the Evolution of the Human Mind
by John McCrone

132 - Friday, November 16, 2007

"... to the uninitiated marvelous gibberish ..."
Myth of Invariance: The Origins of the Gods,
Mathematics and Music from the Rg Veda to Plato
by Ernest G. McClain

134 - Sunday, November 18, 2007

Do go get a copy of this book ...
Do-Gooders: How Liberals Hurt Those
They Claim to Help (and the Rest of Us)
by Mona Charen

136 - Thursday, November 22, 2007

(sigh) ... what to say?
**Out of the Blue:
The Remarkable Story of the 2003 Chicago Cubs**
by Chicago Tribune

138 - Wednesday, November 28, 2007

Well ...
**The Ancient Ones:
Sacred Monuments of the Inka, Maya & Cliffdweller**
by Hans Li

140 - Sunday, December 2, 2007

Skipping ahead here ...
Dada: Art and Anti-Art
by Hans Richter

142 - Saturday, December 15, 2007

Still skipping ahead ...
Delhi and its Neighbourhood
by Y.D. Sharma

144 - Saturday, December 15, 2007

"The earth is all conceivable pain compacted into a single point."
**The Comedy of Agony:
A Book of Poisonous Contemplations**
by Christopher Spranger

147 - Thursday, December 20, 2007

Ninjas! ...
Secrets Of The Ninja
by Ashida Kim

149 - Tuesday, December 25, 2007

Ho, ho, ho ...
The God Delusion
by Richard Dawkins

152 - Saturday, December 29, 2007

Long time for this one ...
Legendary Britain: An Illustrated Journey
by Bob Stewart & John Matthews

154 - Monday, January 31, 2007

A grim read ...
Germs: Biological Weapons and America's Secret War
by Judith Miller, Stephen Engelberg & William Broad

157 - **QR Code Links**

179 - **Contents - Alphabetical By Author**

187 - **Contents - Alphabetical By Title**

Monday, January 1, 2007[1]

A very good book ...

O.K., so I know that my Liberal readers are *already* feeling their panties knot up, so let me at least throw them a bone before getting into looking at this book. It *is possible* to lay the blame for everything that has gone bad with the media over the past 30-some years at the feet of the "evil corporate executives" running the companies that own CBS, NBC, ABC, etc. ... one of the first things I bookmarked in this was a story from the early 70's where a "good news/bad news" report was being made at a staff meeting at CBS ... both of which were that the CBS News division had made a profit for the first quarter in its history, and everybody in the room knew that once that happened, it would be *expected* to continue to happen.

In times of fast-breaking events, even the most slanted news vehicles can rise to the occasion and actually *report the news* as it happens, but in a profit-driven corporate culture, the "if it bleeds, it leads" school takes over, sensationalizing and "spinning" every story. What long-time CBS News reporter Bernard Goldberg points out in Bias: A CBS Insider Exposes How the Media Distort the News[2] is that the *people* managing what shows up on the air (and, to a large extent, in the newspapers) are not only "sensationalism" driven, but live in a "liberal bubble" world where middle-American conservatism is never seriously considered (a great quote in there was from a New York reporter who was shocked by Nixon's election, *carrying 49 states*, saying "nobody *I know* voted for him!").

Goldberg touches on a lot of very "dangerous" topics in the course of this book, from looking at "racial quotas" on what sort of faces get on videotape (not showing videotapes of looting in Haiti because there were no *White* looters to show in a 98% Black country!), to demands of "minority" voices being sources for every story run by many newspapers (with the frustration of reporters to find a black Jew to interview for a Hanukah story in Oklahoma, or this one Asian lady who was interviewed numerous times a month on widely divergent topics, just because she was a "non-white" in her community). On this level, Goldberg is almost more "sad" than angry ... but it borders on the bizarre when the producers *demand* "attractive white middle class faces" when dealing with stories about Alabama chain gangs, crack houses, and homeless families.

This last topic is of particular interest, as Goldberg shows how a "social issue" can pretty much disappear over-night depending on who is in the White House. From standard studies showing head counts of a few hundred thousand homeless, the media drove up these figures to as high as *19 million* (in a Charles Osgood feature, no less). Then, suddenly, the "homeless problem" seemingly ceased to exist ... for eight years it dropped off the radar of the major media. What happened? Did homelessness simply go away? Not exactly, but the answer lies in the chapter *"How Bill Clinton Cured Homelessness"*... simply by not having a Republican in office to bash with whatever issue was at hand, the question of homelessness was suddenly not a "useful story", until about three weeks into G.W.B.'s Presidency, when suddenly, all these homeless were back in the news. Tied into this is a look at how the Mainstream Media will print virtually *any* press release from extreme Left "activist" groups (no doubt where that 19,000,000 figure came from) without even a gesture of fact-checking *{Earth calling Dan Rather}*, but will blatantly disregard anything coming from a source more to the Right than their own insular opinions.

Goldberg is, if anything, easy on his old colleagues, he *understands* "where they're coming from", and had been a long-time Liberal stalwart himself. In fact the entire trigger for the events detailed in Bias[3] come from an opinion piece he wrote about a story on CBS when Steve Forbes was running for the Republican nomination. The news story was sneering, nasty, and belittling of Forbes' (very good) Flat-Tax platform, and Goldberg wrote his piece chastising his fellow CBS employees for providing a serious *disservice* to their viewers in simply slamming the man an his ideas, rather than examining them. It is amazing to see how quickly he was being painted as being somewhere to the right of Rush Limbaugh!

Of course, Goldberg runs the risk of being compared to Ann Coulter when he starts quoting Lexis/Nexis figures for news coverage. The Left always screams bloody murder when Ann points out the hefty Liberal slant on stories appearing the media, and I'm sure this is likely to rub off on anybody else pointing out the transparency of the emperors' suit. However, Goldberg backs up his assertions with solid facts and figures, and I can only imagine the lefties sticking their fingers in their ears and going "nah, nah, nah, nah, I can't hear you" to avoid these uncomfortable truths.

Needless to say, I *highly recommend* picking up a copy of Bernard Goldberg's Bias[4]! It is still in print (in both hardcover and paperback), so should be available through your local store, but it can also be had via the Amazon new/used vendors for as little as a penny (I picked up a virtually pristine copy of the hardcover for 1¢!), with "new" copies starting just under a buck!

Again, this is one that I think *everybody* should read ... even the Liberals, who might get some sense of why when they open their mouths the rest of us look at them like they need to put in a rubber room!

Notes:

1. http://btripp-books.livejournal.com/28145.html
2-4. http://amzn.to/29VDdSv

Tuesday, January 16, 2007[1]

Back to the books ...

This is an odd one to try to review ... The Equinox, Volume III, Number 10[2] as edited by "Hymenaeus Beta X°" is something of a classic (even though only published in 1986), as it pulls together most of the "foundation documents" of the O.T.O., Aleister Crowley's *Ordo Templi Orientis*. Often attributed *to* Crowley (who died nearly 40 years prior to its publication), this appears to be a compilation designed by the modern leaders of the O.T.O. to serve as a focus for who they are and what they're about.

While perhaps a bit over half the book *are* pieces penned by Crowley, either directly, or under his various esoteric *noms de guerre* (Master Therion, Baphomet XI°, etc.), it is much more an "O.T.O. Book" than a "Crowley book", and it's confusing that many (such as amazon.com) insist on listing this as "by Crowley" (to their defense, a different edition of this book than the one I have does say, in rather large letters, "Aleister Crowley" on the cover) whereas much of the book is by others, and even of quite recent vintage.

This volume is a late addition (Vol. 3, No. 10) to the over-all work The Equinox[3] ("The Review of Scientific Illuminism") started by Crowley in 1909. For its first few years, new editions came out twice a year, which then had a substantial gap (after Vol 2 went unreleased), and slowed to every five or six years up to Crowley's death in 1947. Since then new editions have come out sporadically, although the court victories for the O.T.O. in 1985 (over a competing organization headed by Marcelo Motta) seem to have spurred a new cycle of publication via Weiser.

As you are probably suspecting (given the non-specifics of the text), this all does not necessarily present itself as an engrossing read. It swings wildly, from such core texts as Crowley's "channeled" *Book Of The Law* and the O.T.O. *Gnostic Mass* to detailed reports about the 1985 lawsuits, with stops at theoretical organizational structures for lodges, etc. (from 1919), and an entire section dealing with the films of Kenneth Anger, sprinkled with some random poetry, essays, and a bit of fiction.

I suppose that if one was somewhat interested in the O.T.O. (and there are quite a number of very active O.T.O. members around LiveJournal), The Equinox, Volume III, Number 10[4] would be a decent place to start, although there are quite impressive archives of the key materials available on the web (such as at hermetic.com[5]). This does appear to still be in print, so you could likely find it at your local bookstore. Oddly enough, there don't seem to be any used "deals" on this, as Amazon's new/used vendor listings for it come in only slightly less than Amazon's discounted price, so if this sounds like something you'd want to add to your collection, I guess that's the best you're going to get.

Notes:
http://btripp-books.livejournal.com/28246.html
http://amzn.to/29VBnB4
http://en.wikipedia.org/wiki/The_Equinox
http://amzn.to/29VBnB4
http://www.hermetic.com/crowley/index.html

Wednesday, January 17, 2007[1]

Back-to-back reviews, eh?

There were actually several days in between finishing that last book and this one, but I was dragging my feet on the previous review, and had a feeling that I should get this out before the details fade.

Shabono: A Visit to a Remote and Magical World in the South American Rain Forest[2] by Florinda Donner is an easy, interesting read ... but one of those that you stand back from and somewhat wonder about. First of all, the author purports to be the "Florinda" of the Castaneda books, one of the sorcerers in Don Juan Matus' circle. As I understand it, Castaneda acknowledged her (and Taisha Abelar) while denying the claims of several others, but I've also seen various things on the web (admittedly, from what seem to be disgruntled students) which raise a lot of questions of how this author could have been in the places she claims to have been, with the people she writes about, at the times that the various events were said to take place.

As I've written about Sufi books (and especially those of Idries Shah), you often need to try to see the intent behind a book before you can judge on what level the book is meant to operate. This is frequently the case for Shamanic books as well, where the inner dynamics are more important than the "historical accuracy" of the narrative. My own Shamanic teacher, Alberto Villoldo, would drop a file box full of notes off to his co-author and pretty much leave it to the unfortunate writer to piece together a book (which, from my own experience, often results in a tale that's nothing like the actual timeline of events covered), and perhaps something similar is in effect here. If we suspend doubt and take Ms. Donner as who she supposedly is, Shabono[3] is still a pretty vague book, very dream-like in its presentation, with descriptions of people, places, and things which *suggest* but hardly present clear images. Of course, at a relatively early point in the story, she *does* let us know how her notes (what the natives referred to as her "decorating" her paper) got destroyed, so there *is* an excuse in that the whole tale is crafted from after-the-fact recall.

Given these caveats, this is still a book worth reading. The story is of the author's time staying with a *Yanomama* tribal group in the vast jungles of South America; the title comes from their word for a settlement or village. She starts out as an anthropologist doing research into the healing methods of various "medicine people" in Venezuela, and is invited to accompany some friends on a trip up the Orinoco River, where she hopes to possibly meet a native Shaman. Rather abruptly (in terms of continuity), she gets to a river outpost, and dis-engages from the rest of traveling group, connects with a very old Yanomama lady, and (against all warnings) goes off with her to visit her village. What was supposed to have been a 2-week trip then turns into a year of living among the natives where she eventually gets her "Shamanic experience" but hardly in the ways she expected. Again, I felt the narrative was a bit lean on concrete descriptions, and many details seemed like they were added in after having been looked up in books on the flora and fauna of the region. Even the "shamanic" parts seemed "off" to me, but this could well be due to the rather idiosyncratic concept of *hekuras* (little "spirit people") that she indicates are at the center of the native shamanic practice, with which I don't have any direct parallel to fairly compare.

This does appear to still be in print, so you might be able to get it via your local bookstore, but Amazon has it for 1/3 off of cover, and their new/used vendors (which is where I got *mine*) have "like new" copies for as little as a buck and a half (plus shipping), should you decide that a lazy mental drift up the Orinoco is appealing.

Notes:

1. http://btripp-books.livejournal.com/28431.html
2-3. http://amzn.to/2a3WNew

Saturday, January 20, 2007[1]

Better late than never, I guess ...

I've been *finally* getting around to reading some of the Kalachakra books I've had up on the shelf for ages. I'm not sure *when* exactly I got these, but I suspect (judging from publication dates, etc.) that I picked them up at my third Kalachakra Initiation in New York back in 1991. A couple of years after I got out of college I sort of "fell into" Vajrayana as I had friends doing grad work up in Madison, WI and the first ever[2] Kalachakra to be given outside of India or Tibet was going to be happening up there to launch the Deer Park center. I was assured that this was *a very big deal* and encouraged to attend. Well, between July of 1981 and October of 1991, I took the Kalachakra Initiation three times (Madison '81, Los Angeles '89, and New York '91) and the Avalokiteśvara Initiation twice (Madison '8?, Los Angeles '84), but didn't really start getting around to "studying" it until the last one, and at that point I sort of disengaged from all that, despite having purchased a number of books on the subject.

I've previously expressed regret that I hadn't read some of these books *before* one of the initiations, and Geshe Sopa's The Wheel of Time: The Kalachakra in Context[3] is certainly like that ... I would have definitely gotten *a lot* more out of these experiences had I had the "framing" of some of these books ... unfortunately, the timing just wasn't there for me! This book is credited to Geshe Lhundub Sopa, who is the director of Deer Park up in Madison, but it is actually a collection of several essays by him and a couple of western students (with a foreword by the Dalai Lama) on various aspects of the Kalachakra.

Now, if you've not encountered Vajrayana Buddhism (which would be most people), it's very much based on visualizations (as I've often joked, most Tibetan Buddhism comes from guys who spent years in tiny cells on mountainsides staring at a blank wall), and to *fully* "get" the Kalachakra Initiation:

> "One is said to have accomplished the generation stage of the Kalachakra when one can visualize the entire mandala in a drop the size of a mustard seed at the tip of one's nose, with such clarity that one can see the whites of the eyes of all 722 deities - and can maintain this visualization with uninterrupted one-pointed concentration for four hours."

... needless to say, few (of the thousands who attend these events) come even *close* to having that level of practice! However, the Dalai Lama has said that one of the reasons for doing such large ceremonies (the ones I attended had about 3,000 but some of the Indian ones have had over 200,000 there!) is to provide the necessary karmic connections to students who in a previous existence had *done the work* but had not been able to attend an initiation to get the "permissions" (on a mystical level) to unlock the practice.

One thing that I had not "gotten" from attending these was the "prophetic" nature of parts of the Kalachakra tradition. Now, "kalachaka" translates to "wheel of time", so this is not a *big* surprise, but I found it fascinating to see some of the specifics. One of the prophesies involves the near-destruction of the Dharma by "the barbarians", a group that closely parallels the Muslims, with the "mantra of the barbarian deity" being *bi si mi lla*, remarkably close to the Arabic *bismillah*, "in the name of Allah", and the "name of the barbarian deity" being *rahma na*, similar to *al-Rahman*, "the Merciful", an Islamic name for God ... thankfully the prophesies end up well, with armies from Shambhala crushing the barbarians and establishing a new golden age.

I've always recommended the Vajrayana visualization practices as a very useful tool in any mystical tradition (I've found the techniques especially useful in Shamanic work), so this is a book that might give you some ideas, even if you're not particularly interested in the esoterica of Tibetan Buddhism! The Wheel of Time[4] is still in print, so you should be able to get it from your local bookstore, although "new" copies are available via the Amazon new/used vendors for somewhat over half of current cover price.

Notes:

1. http://btripp-books.livejournal.com/28774.html
2. http://www.dalailama.com/page.22.htm
3-4. http://amzn.to/29QiGhW

Wednesday, January 24, 2007[1]

Can't say much about this one ...

Yep, catching up on more of the Kalachakra reading I've had sitting around since the 80's ... this one is interesting in that it's listed as for "Restricted Sale", officially only available to those who (like me) who have taken the Kalachakra Initiation. This is the case for this (the 1985) edition, but it seems that there was a 1998 re-issue (which is where the ISBN comes from), and I'm not sure if that restriction was still in place. However, I feel that I have to respect this, so am going to be somewhat more vague on details than usual here.

The book Kalacakra Tantra[2] (yes, spelled here without the "h") evolved out of a series of talks that Geshe Ngawang Dhargyey presented at the Sakya Tegchen Choling center in Seattle over a couple of months in early 1982, following the first Kalachakra Initiation (Madison, WI in July '81). H.H. the Dalai Lama had encouraged the Geshe to travel to the U.S. to present background materials for students of the Vajrayana, and this was the result.

While I'm not sure what is so "secret" about the content of this, as compared to other books on the Kalachakra, it certainly was an eye-opener as far as plain talk about various things which all too often are presented in "symbolic" terms. It also is very up front about specific things to watch for in one's practice, and how to avoid various pitfalls. This was, of course, a fascinating glimpse into what it must be like to be working on these practices in a monastic setting.

Again, this presentation came from the very early days of the Kalachakra's spread to the west (prior to 1981 it had never been given outside of India or Tibet), and the Geshe keeps touching back on the points of how *fortunate* we are as Westerners to be able to have fairly easy access to high Lamas (such as my having been able to have taken *five* initiations, despite having virtually *no* background in "practice", from His Holiness the Dalai Lama), where in its native land, most lay practitioners would have had extreme difficulties in attaining this sort of contact, if they could manage it at all.

While this is *listed* on the Library of Tibetan Works and Archives (its publisher) publication page, it does not appear to currently be officially for sale, although there *are* copies available (both of this 1985 edition and the 1998 version) at a substantial mark-up via the Amazon new/used vendors were one to wish to obtain a copy.

Notes:

1. http://btripp-books.livejournal.com/29152.html
2. http://amzn.to/2ao2LWE

Monday, January 29, 2007[1]

That was a long read ...

Whew ... well, *that* took a long time to plow through! To those who have paid attention to my LibraryThing listings[2], you will notice a certain periodicity in the logging in of science books. This is because I tend to have one "going" at any given time (over by the "reading chair" in my office), while reading other stuff in other locations, and typically starting up a new one right on the heels of the last finished[*]. So, that means that I've been working on Kip Thorne's Black Holes and Time Warps: Einstein's Outrageous Legacy[3] for *seven weeks*, which is a very long time for me to be tied up with any given book. Of course, this was a longer book than most (officially over 600 pages), but it was also pretty dense (especially in the early parts where he was laying the theoretical groundwork on which to build the later material) and as often as not, I ended up nodding off after a couple of pages' reading!

Now, this is not to cast aspersions on Dr. Thorne's prose, or the interest level of his subjects, just noting that this was not exactly a speedy "page turner" ... I often envy fiction readers their easy tasks, but figure that life is too short not to read serious books (if I want fantasy, I have the SciFi channel!).

Frankly, I'm guessing that this must be used as a college text, as it appears in a lot more users' libraries on L.T. than many more accessible physics books. It is an interesting and ambitious venture ... starting off with Einstein's work and showing how those various theories were developed upon over the years, with particular emphasis on the evolution of the concept of "black holes" and various radio sources. One of the ongoing efforts Thorne makes in the book is to try to give a "visual sense" of assorted 4-D concepts, charted out in 2-D representations of 3-D models ... a challenge with the simplest diagrams, and nearly impossible for some of the more convoluted versions of curved space/time! Thorne puts a lot of the theory in context by way of "fleshing out" the scientists responsible for the concepts. He especially provides an interesting sketch of Soviet science in its somewhat-parallel development during the Cold War.

There were several *fascinating* bits in Black Holes and Time Warps[4] that I had either not encountered or at least not registered previously, such as that *all* sub-atomic particles share the same sort of wave/particle dual nature that is more commonly known for the photon, plus there are some very interesting, almost "fractal" recurrences of sets of physical laws (like classical thermodynamics) in completely unexpected theoretical settings. This also whetted my appetite for more info on the Planck-Wheeler length, area, and time ... an amazing set of concepts/equations that brings reality down to the smallest possible gauges (at 10^{-33}cm, where *"space has become a froth of probabilistic quantum foam"*).

Now, this is yet another of those physics books that I've had sitting around for *ages*, having come out in 1994 ... so a lot of the "raw cutting edge" bits in here have likely been eclipsed by other research, and there are, no doubt, many answers for stuff left hanging in this. However, unlike some of the other older physics books I've read recently, this doesn't feel as dated ... probably because Thorne was operating in a specialization which wasn't waiting for the SSC to come on line.

There is a paperback version of this that is still in print, so you should be able to find it locally. Amazingly (for such an obscure topic), there aren't any "dirt cheap" copies out there, but you could get a "very good" copy for about half of what Amazon's charging for a new one (which also makes me think these are in the textbook market). It is fascinating stuff, if you're into physics, and there's info in this that I've not found elsewhere, so could well be worth your while.

*Although this particular pattern is breaking in that my next book in "that slot" is a hefty large-format book on Tibetan art that I bought back in '91 when I was in NYC for the Kalachakra.

Notes:

1. http://btripp-books.livejournal.com/29379.html
2. http://btripp-books.com/
3-4. http://amzn.to/29Vz418

Tuesday, February 13, 2007[1]

One last (I think) on the Kalachakra ...

This, I believe (you never know what might be lurking in boxes of unread books around here), catches me up on the various books I've had sitting around for 15 years on the Kalachakra, most of which (if memory serves) I picked up at the New York City initiation back in 1991.

Glenn H. Mullin's The Practice of Kalachakra[2] was published in '91, and is a solid over-view of the Kalachakra, both putting it in context of history and the Vajrayana Buddhist tradition, and supplying key historical texts. Mullin is a prolific translator/interpreter of Tibetan texts, and is affiliated with the Library of Tibetan Works and Archives, and in this volume he does both, the first half being an exposition of the Kalachakra's history, and the second being eight texts from leading Lamas, including several of the incarnations of the Dalai Lama (the 1st, 7th, 13th, and the current 14th).

While this book is not "restricted", I still find it hard to cogently write something about the *content* per se, simply because of the complexity of the subject. Where does one start? Buddhism is an evolving faith, with aspects that are strongly counter-intuitive to the Western mind (for instance, within the Kalachakra materials it is given that the historical Buddha taught the Kalachakra at the request of the King of Shambhala somewhere around 500bce, but the teachings were only preserved in Shambhala for the first thousand years after the time of the Buddha, and didn't reappear in the *mundane* world until the first millennium of the common era). Plus, from the Tibetan view, there are progressives layers of "paths", with the Sutrayana, Mantrayana, Tanrayana, and Vajrayana (expanding on the usual Hinayana/Mahayana division), each becoming more technical, but including the previous approaches.

As I've noted in previous reviews on the subject, the Kalachakra is unusual in that, while being from the highest levels of Vajrayana practices, it has been (at least in recent times) generally presented in large gatherings where anybody can attend. The reason for this has been explained that for these Tantric practices "to work", one *must* be given ritual permissions, and there have been countless beings who have *practiced* the Kalachakra over the centuries, but very few who were able to make the difficult journey to a major monastic center to actually go through the initiations. By allowing any and all to attend (and some of these in India have had a quarter million people show up!) it is felt that those who have karmic ties to the Kalachakra can, retroactively, get the necessary permissions, hopefully leading to enlightenment.

Speaking of enlightenment, it has occurred to me that what appeals to many Westerners about the Kalachakra, is that it is (within its context) the "quick path". While other paths might hold that practice over numerous lifetimes may bring one to a rebirth in a favorable setting for enlightenment, the Kalachakra claims to provide a way to full enlightenment in this lifetime, and even within a "doable" window of time within one's current lifetime. Not that this is an "easy way", as the effective practice of Kalachakra requires one to encompass virtually all of the regimens and prescriptions of the preceding paths, and it necessitates a level of mental concentration that is not easily attained. However, I do think that the prospect that "if I really work intensely at this for the next 10-15 years I'll achieve this" is quite alluring to those of us in the West for whom the concept of cyclic rebirths is somewhat alien!

Anyway, if this sounds interesting to you (karmic connections?), you may want to check out The Practice of Kalachakra[3], as it will certainly give you a good basis in what the Kalachakra is about. This is still in print, but there don't seem to be a lot of "deals" available for it, so your best bet is probably a sale off of retail (like one of those Borders or B&N coupons for 20% off a single item).

Notes:

1. http://btripp-books.livejournal.com/29687.html

2-3. http://amzn.to/29HirqW

Saturday, February 17, 2007[1]

Dalai Lama ...

What can I say about this? Over the past 30 years, the biographical outline of the current Dalai Lama has been very familiar to me, so much of this was a "filling in the details". Of course, you (my intrepid readers, such as there are), may not be as conversant with the story, so I guess an over-view would be in order.

Freedom In Exile: the Autobiography of the Dalai Lama[2] is just that, the current (14th) Dalai Lama's telling of his life story, from his birth in 1935 in the north-eastern provinces of Tibet through 1990 (when the first edition of this came out). In the Tibetan Buddhist tradition, certain high Lamas (referred to as *Tulkus*) are able to re-incarnate in identifiable forms to continue their teachings, the Dalai Lamas are one such lineage, of which Tenzin Gyatso is the fourteenth manifestation. Over the past 400 or so years, the Dalai Lamas have been both the leaders of the Tibetan nation as well as the head of the Gelugpa order.

It was said that his predecessor had seen visions of the great trials that the Tibetan people would go through with the rise of Communism in China and had "died early" in order that his reincarnated form would have a chance to be ready for those events. As it was, the current Dalai Lama was only 15 years old (with the government being run via a Regency) when the Chinese invaded in 1950. The next decade was very turbulent, with the Chinese encroaching more and more on the Tibetan way of life. Finally, in 1959, the Dalai Lama had to flee the country, re-settling (eventually with many refugees) in India.

While the Chinese destruction of Tibet's unique culture is a massive tragedy, the Tibetan diaspora has resulted in the wide spread of their particular form of Buddhism, which might not have taken root all over the world the way it has were Tibet to have survived as it had been for the previous thousand years. Needless to say, I would have been very unlikely to have crossed paths with Vajrayana without it, rather than having had the opportunity to have taken *five* initiations from the Dalai Lama here in the U.S. between 1981 and 1991!

Freedom In Exile[3] goes into the details of how the Dalai Lama dealt with this upheaval, and struggled with political structures that were willing to "throw Tibet under the bus" rather than challenge the Chinese. While, frankly, there was precious little The West could have practically done to keep the Chinese out of Tibet, it would have been nice had there been more willingness to stand up to the forces of evil rather than simply ignoring them (but what can you expect when the American Congress even *now* is wanting to hide under the covers and pretend that the whole world would be out singing *Kumbaya* if we quit fighting organized terror!). The Nobel Peace Prize that was awarded to the Dalai Lama in 1989 hardly makes right the butchery of hundreds of thousands of Tibetans and the wanton destruction of thousands of irreplaceable monasteries (and the centuries of learning/

tradition that had been preserved in them) when the Chinese artillery came into play.

In any event, this is an interesting volume on several levels, there is the whole "Tibetan" historical angle, the coming of age of a young man in a very imposing role, and the global political tale that weaves through the narrative, with some fascinating observations made first-hand of Mao and other Chinese leaders, Nehru and other Indian leaders, etc. Freedom In Exile[4] is still in print, so should be available at your local bookstore, but Amazon has it for about $11 new, and "like new" copies from the new/used vendors going for about $5.00. If you have an interest in religion, in gripping autobiographies, and of modern socio-political history, this is certainly one to consider picking up!

Notes:

1. http://btripp-books.livejournal.com/29843.html

2-4. http://amzn.to/2a3RNGS

Saturday, February 17, 2007[1]

More Tibet ...

I've had this book for a *very* long time. It used to sit out on one of the coffee tables in my old apartment (which I've not lived in for something like 15 years), which is why the dust cover is a bit bleached out. Oddly enough, I never actually bothered to *read* it all those years, preferring to flip through the fascinating antique photos.

Tibet: The Sacred Realm - Photographs 1880-1950[2] is an amazing collection of the early Western views of the classic Buddhist kingdom of Tibet. So much of what is pictured in here is gone, swept away by the crushing insanity of the Chinese communists, from the thuggish invasion of 1950 to the attempted total obliteration of Tibetan culture during China's disastrous "Cultural Revolution" in the late '60s and early '70s.

The part of this that I missed (while focusing solely on the pictures) is a very interesting look at the later days of the "old Tibet". Actually, it was probably a good thing that I waited to read this "chronicle" by lama and Tibetan government official Lobsang P. Lhalungpa until *after* I finished reading the Dalai Lama's Freedom In Exile[3], as this story fleshes out parts of that autobiography with details that would have been very difficult for the Dalai Lama to know, due to his position. Lobsang P. Lhalungpa discusses the general outline of his own life story, including his education and advancement into the government, but also discusses many social and cultural aspects of Tibetan life that I had not seen explored before. His story ends a bit differently, though, as he was selected to manage a Tibetan school already set up in India, and left for that posting in 1947, although even at that time the fateful events of 1950 were hovering over the horizon. Both his narrative and the time-line of the photographs end in 1950, the year the Communist Chinese army swept in and changed things forever in his homeland.

The book also features a brief Preface by The 14th Dalai Lama His Holiness Tenzin Gyatso, which is interesting in that it is in Tibetan script (H.H.'s handwriting?), with English translations line-by-line. While this was written in 1982 when the Dalai Lama had already been to the U.S.A. (and other Western sites), one gets a sense that he had not quite gotten to the "communication comfort" level that he would eventually have in penning his autobiography some eight years later.

Additionally, there is a final section in the book which does a little biographical sketch of all the photographers whose work appears in the book, presenting something of a "who's who" of Oriental adventurers, from Alexandra David-Neel (author of Magic and Mystery in Tibet[4], among many others) to the well-known Heinrich Harrer (author of Seven Years in Tibet[5] detailing his WW2 escape from a British internment camp in India and ending up as a "Western tutor" to the young Dalai Lama *(by the way, this can be had for as little as 2¢ for a "like new" copy right now!)*), and many other military and visionary travelers in between.

This original 1983 edition of Tibet: The Sacred Realm[6] is no longer available (well, one of the new/used guys looks like they may have it, but they want over eighty bucks for a "very good" copy!), but can be had via the used market in either the 1990 re-issue of the hardcover ("like new" for $14.00) or the 1997 paperback (a "new" copy for as little as $9.95). This is really a remarkable collection of pictures, and would be well worth picking it up via those options (both well under the original cover price).

Notes:

1. http://btripp-books.livejournal.com/30200.html
2. http://amzn.to/29PdsWy
3. http://btripp-books.livejournal.com/29843.html
4. http://amzn.to/2egA3Ki
5. http://amzn.to/2eBEvUy
6. http://amzn.to/29PdsWy

Sunday, February 25, 2007

I should have read the title ...

OK, so I was amused (when I finally got around to *reading* this book) at the fact that I was *surprised* that the book was primarily about *mountain climbing*! This is another of my old "coffee table books" that I used to have out in my previous apartment (some 15+ years ago), largely for its very cool images of Tibet (most notably, the awesome cover shot of a huge rainbow smacking right into the Potala).

I mean, I *might* have gotten a clue from the sub-title in Mountains of the Middle Kingdom: Exploring the High Peaks of China and Tibet[2] that adventure photojournalist Galen Rowell was actually talking *mountaineering*, rather than "just poking around up in the mountains and taking awesome pictures", which, needless to say, was *my* mental image (after all, one would be "exploring" amid the "high peaks" just to be up in Tibet). As such, I learned a lot about stuff to which I'd had no previous exposure (although, admittedly, it did take me a while to stop wondering why the author seemed so clueless about Vajrayana Buddhism!).

Actually, the book is an interesting window into "the Chinese side" of a lot of Tibetan issues, as Rowell seems to have far more exposure to that than to the "international Tibetan community". Lots of pretty pictures of mountains, nomads, and (less pretty) ruined monasteries. He does note that out of the 3,000 or so Tibetan monasteries in existence before the Chinese invasion, only a scant handful survived the insanity of "The Cultural Revolution", and these are the current "Disneyland-like" tourist spots operated by the Chinese in the interest of hard currency.

The book swings back and forth between historical information on who climbed which peak when and how, and his own experiences on or around the various mountains. To be honest, I'd only heard of one of these (Everest, *duh!*), but the "adventure" stories were fascinating. The take-away that a desk slug like me gets, though, is that climbing up a mountain is a real good way to get dead in various (none particularly pleasant) ways. Heck, even attempting to *get to* most of these mountains was traditionally an invitation to have your guts removed and eyes torn out, while today you'll just be bureaucracied to death, and charged 10x what the going rate would be on the Nepal side of the hill.

The pictures in Mountains of the Middle Kingdom[3] are, of course, *spectacular*. Rowell is a frequent *National Geographic* contributor, and certainly knows how to drag the best image out of a vista. That cover shot, by the way, wasn't photoshopped or anything ... He *ran* out on a road heading away from the Potala in Lhasa just to get to the place where this amazing rainbow would look like it was coming right down on the Dalai Lama's old palace. Frankly Rowell and his associates do *way* too much high-altitude running for my liking (I was getting winded just *reading* about it), but if it gets shots like the one on the cover, I guess it can't be all bad.

This does appear to be out of print currently, so if you want a copy, you're at the mercy of the new/used vendors (and even there, it's slim pickings), with $10.00 getting you a "very good" copy, and around $20.00 for "like new". Part of the problem with this is that it's a large format (12"w by 10"h) paperback, which is always an invitation for bends, curls, and edge-wear. It's a great picture book, though, and would no doubt be a gripping read for outdoorsy types!

Notes:

1. http://btripp-books.livejournal.com/30322.html

2-3. http://amzn.to/29Tvvcv

Thursday, March 1, 2007[1]

A long read ...

This is a *massive* book, large format (9x12"), hardcover, heavy "art" pages, very impressive. It was done to accompany a major Tibetan art exhibit back in 1991 in New York, at the same time as the Kalachakra Initiation. It seems to me that I did get a chance to see the exhibit, and may have bought this there (or may have gotten it a a discount ... from the $75 cover price! ... for Kalachakra participants at the event). Anyway, it has sat around for quite a while, and was the last of the things from then I had had to plow through.

One would think that a big, beautiful book like Wisdom and Compassion: The Sacred Art of Tibet[2] would make for a relatively easy read ... being that it is at least half *pictures*, but, of course, there is very little "flow", and a lot of technical detail, and it really did become quite a chore to grind through (especially since I kept nodding off). However, I now know a vast lot more about Tibetan art than I did before, which I guess is a good thing. While not encyclopedic, this will give anybody a good grounding in the subject, and has many references off to more in-depth studies, if one was so inclined.

The book starts off with various introductory bits and then moves into a several essays putting the material in context regarding history, religion, and artistic styles. The bulk of the book is broken up into three main segments, "Tibetan Sacred History", "Tibetan Buddhist Orders", and "Tibetan Perfect Worlds", each of which is sub-divided into various subject areas. So, instead dealing with a whole section on statuary, a whole section on paintings, etc., each subject has an array of pieces relating to it. The book then closes with another essay on the artistic techniques used.

Now, Art was one of my three majors in college, but I was never much of a fan of Art History, so (as fascinating as I found many of the pieces in here from a *religion* standpoint), this did drag on for me, and I'm real glad I didn't have to write a final paper or take an exam on it! However, if you like "studying" art, this is a goldmine.

And, unfortunately, it will take some gold to get a copy ... as this started out at seventy-five bucks, the used copies (there don't seem to be any "new" ones to be had in either the 1991 original or the 2000 "expanded" edition) run anywhere from $60 all the way up to $250! ... so you pretty much need to have a burning desire to learn about this stuff to get in on this. It's a great addition to anybody's library, though ... just not an easy read or a cheap acquisition!

Notes:

1. http://btripp-books.livejournal.com/30716.html
2. http://amzn.to/2anUVwa

Thursday, March 8, 2007[1]

This started out well ...

OK, let me get one snarky comment out of the way before delving into this book ... in the section on Chinese medicine, this lists "the seven human emotions" as "joy, anger, melancholy, brooding, sorrow, fear and shock". I never realized how *Chinese* I must be ... a 6-1 ratio of negativity! Go me, eh?

Healing and the Mind[2] is a book by TV reporter Bill Moyers, which appears to be a "companion volume" to a PBS series from the early 90's by the same name. I don't recall ever seeing the TV version, so I was coming to this fresh (if 15 years late). Organized in five sections (with various chapters focusing on interviews with individual doctors and researchers), it "peaks out" early, with the first three building a *fascinating* examination of "what causes healing" (including some amazing research on how intention and mental states can dramatically effect what's happening to the body on a microscopic level), but then "falls off the table" with a long *"gee whiz, they do everything different there!"* look at Chinese medicine (revealing little not commonly known to folks conversant with metaphysical topics), and then closing with a pointless section with two maudlin chapters looking at *one* small "cancer group" which offers *nothing* towards the thesis of the book.

This could have been a Very Important Book had it continued building on the first three sections rather than essentially abandoning the thrust built there to chase after "exotica" and "emotional content". The book initially makes a very potent case for meditation, ritual, and (by implication) things like hypnotism and shamanic work, and contrasts that with the western "medical orthodoxy". It makes me wonder if "political forces" came to bear to switch the focus here, as Moyers was getting very directed at some of the *real* under-lying issues with our Health services ... as an example, here's what Dean Ornish had to say at one point: *"The insurance industry is really the major determinant of health care in this country - not science and not clinical experience, but what a third party will pay for."* ... it was repeatedly noted that *hundreds* of people can be taught basic preventative exercises (focused meditations in the guise of a "stress reduction" clinic) a year for far less than the costs of a single operation, but still the money isn't there to do the prevention. Oh, wait ... how about we go to China?

At least the Chinese section had *some* focus on the mind/body issue (although Moyers seemed to have a very hard time dealing with the concept of "chi"), but the final section was either there to pad out a contracted number of episodes, or was particularly connected with Moyers. Both of the final chapters dealt with a small program where people dying of cancer get together for a few days' retreat, and form a "therapeutic group" which often makes it easier for them to deal with death. I'm sorry, but for a book that starts out showing how mental states can completely change biochemistry, ending up with two chapters of cancer victims singing "Amazing Grace" is just pitiful.

That being said, I still have to recommend this book *for* the first three sections, which are well worth reading. If you have *no clue* about traditional Chinese medicine, I guess the fourth section is OK, but just skip the last part, as it really ruins what starts out as a very good book! This does still seem to be in print (in a reprint paperback), but you can get "very good" copies for as little as a penny from the Amazon new/used vendors, which is what I'd recommend. My copy was from my Mom's place (still shrink-wrapped) and was no doubt left over from some promotion that our local PBS station had done back in '93 (given that it has the ISBN of the initial hardcover edition, but is a paperback with no UPC). Again, the stuff in the first three sections of Healing and the Mind[3] is good enough to make the effort worthwhile, and since you could get a "very good" copy for $3.50 delivered, I'd say go for it!

Notes:

1. http://btripp-books.livejournal.com/30860.html

2-3. http://amzn.to/29PaWva

Saturday, March 10, 2007[1]

Finally read this one ...

I wonder what happened to Dick Hoagland ... I mean, for a while there he was all over Art Bell's show, and there were almost weekly updates to his enterprisemission.com web site, then (from where I sit) *nothing*! Sure, it looks like he's been doing conferences and stuff, but there used to be a constant flow of info (and images) that seems to have gone dry.

Over the years, I'd (obviously) been paying attention to the web presence, but had never quite gotten around to reading his book, The Monuments of Mars: a City On the Edge Of Forever[2]. Well, I picked this up (for a penny ... woot!) last summer and finally got it read. Needless to say, I'd known the broad strokes of how Hoagland had been a "media type" around NASA (he was a "space advisor" to Walter Cronkite), and was one of the various folks to glom onto "The Face" formation[3] that the Viking orbiters imaged in the "Cydonia" region of Mars. Well, from this one image (and the area around it), Hoagland and his associates built up quite a "mythology" (of variable levels of believability) about some ancient civilization (quite ancient, by some figures) which had left these huge sculptures (the Face is something like a mile per side) as intentional "signs" for us to see.

Now, I always "glaze over" when folks start going on about "significant" angles and things of that ilk, and much of what Hoagland & Co. base the "unnaturalness" of the Cydonia features is a whole web of these angular alignments. *Personally*, I would be more impressed if everything lined up in a nice even grid that I could take a glance at and say "hey, that's on a grid!", rather than saying (to paraphrase) *"Wow, if you measure from the left nostril of the face to the back corner of this pyramid and then to the trailing edge of this other feature, the angle is 19.5°!!!"*. Admittedly, I have never "gotten" stuff like the Golden Mean (or even musical scales), so this *might* just be playing to my insufficiencies, but the deeper they probe, the less convinced I get.

This is not to say that I don't think that Hoagland & Co. are on to something. His theories merge well with the likes of Sitchin and J.A. West, with which I've previously had a great deal of resonance, but the core issue of this one area on Mars just seems a little weak until we drop a camera right in the middle of it and take a look around.

The Monuments of Mars[4] follows Hoagland from the 1976 "discovery" of the Face through about 1991 (this was an updated 1992 release of the original 1987 book), walking the reader through the "curiouser and curiouser" looks into these "Martian Artifacts", interweaving research streams with others in the same genre, and his "battles" with NASA. One must admit that his struggles with NASA *did* have a certain "X-Files" edge to them, with "official video presentations" being inexplicably edited to remove sections and change dates, etc., but there does seem to be more than a little plain paranoia at play.

Of course, over the years, Hoagland and his team have "branched out" from Cydonia and have questioned all sorts of grainy photos from Mars as to their being "artifacts", and made himself something of a joke in the process (interestingly, in this book he frequently savages Erich von Däniken as having "made things hard for *real* researchers", which, at this remove, sure has a "pot.kettle.black" feel to it!). However, in the process of "all this stuff", I do believe that Hoagland *has* stumbled over some very interesting *physics* that I think are of great importance (see HERE[5] on his site), which I fear may end up doing a "baby with the bathwater" as people dismiss his work in its entirety.

While being more *linear* that the EnterpriseMission site, this book is really best as an introduction to Hoagland's theories, with the real "meat" being on the web (although not recently updated). While an expanded 5th edition of this is currently available, I'm not sure if one would really do better going with a used copy (this version is still available for well under a buck), and "catching up" on his site.

Notes:

1. http://btripp-books.livejournal.com/31028.html
2. http://amzn.to/29Qa22U
3. https://goo.gl/I5ZJ33
4. http://amzn.to/29Qa22U
5. http://www.enterprisemission.com/physics.html

Sunday, March 11, 2007[1]

Not something that I just picked up ...

I have had this odd book sitting around my desk for *ages* ... the other day I was checking back in my LiveJournal "calendar view" to clarify the dates of some things that I was doing just before 9/11/01, and there was a post mentioning this book, so I've be dribbling through this for nearly six years! It has been handy for those occasional "book memes" that say *"grab the nearest book and turn to page ..."* because it's always been good for a juicy quote! Over the past few years I've used it for filling those "this is gong to take a minute or two to download" times, and am now going to have to find something that works as well for that!

Ah, where to start with Ragnar Redbeard's Might is Right: The Survival of the Fittest[2]? Well, first of all, it's an *old* book, variously reported to have been first published in 1890 or 1896, and attributed to any of a half a dozen writers who may or may not have been operating under the cloak of the Redbeard pen name. As one can gather from its title, this is not a "nice" book, and has an unabashed Teutonic chauvinism (with definite anti-Semitic aspects) which can be uncomfortable reading in a post-Nazi era.

If I were to distill the message of Might is Right[3] into a "sound bite", I'd have to borrow a snippet of lyrics from the Sisters of Mercy's tune "More" (and I'm pretty sure that Andrew Eldritch has read this book) which goes *"you won't get what you deserve / **you are what you take**"*. Redbeard has no patience for either priests or politicians, damning equally the emasculating effects of Christianity and the enslaving of the individual by governments (especially the creeping Socialism of his era, now in full vile flower in ours). Of course, to anybody familiar with *my* assorted rants, you would understand how an "anti-Christian/anti-Socialist" message sounds like heavenly choirs to my ears (as I often feel that I'm alone in being a staunch "hawk" conservative who is as anti-Christian as the Beast himself).

There have been many editions of this book over the years (mostly reprints of the 1910 version), put out in various "spins" (the Wikipedia entry for this mentions one that had an introductory essay by Anton LaVey!), including a recent one (currently in print) which has taken a "scholarly" approach and tried to pull together a definitive edition with many footnotes placing the "Victorian" concerns of the author into historical context. The copy I have, however, is the 1999 "Millennial Wotansvolk Edition" from 14-Word Press (a "white power[4]" operation out in Idaho), which is, perhaps, the "most fun" of all of the available versions as it is way "over the top" with Asatru-inspired illustrations and an obvious *enthusiasm* for the author's biases!

I do have to note that to "modern ears" this is a rather *ugly* book, and the author's style is rather dense (not making for a quick read ... but then again, I rarely sat down *to* read this, so it shouldn't take *six years* for most folks to get through its 200 pages). Many will, frankly, find this book *offensive*, and I'd suggest those who are of a Leftist bent, deeply devoted to Christianity, or "touchy" about anti-Semitic stuff, might just pretend it doesn't exist (*"nothing to see here, folks, just keep moving"*)!

Were you interested in picking up a copy of Might Is Right[5], you're in luck that the "scholarly" 2005 edition came out, as a few years ago these were going *used* for over seventy-five bucks, and now a "like new" copy (of the 1999 edition) can be had from the Amazon new/used vendors for around ten bucks (the 2005 version, oddly enough, doesn't currently have any "new/used" offers, so you'd be paying the $13.95 cover for that). Again, keep in mind that this book isn't for most folks, and for every guy who's jumping up and down doing the "kill!" riff from Alice's Restaurant[6] while reading this, there are likely to be 3-4 earnest souls feverishly pounding out letters to their congressmen to have the book banned ... so caveat emptor, as your mileage will doubtlessly vary.

Notes:

1. http://btripp-books.livejournal.com/31478.html
2-3. http://amzn.to/2a5i0aP
4. http://en.wikipedia.org/wiki/Wotanism
5. http://amzn.to/2a5i0aP
6. https://goo.gl/VzdQ6d

Wednesday, March 14, 2007[1]

An odd one ...

As those paying *way* too much attention to this space will recall, I "carry the lineage" of two "Incan" shamanic traditions, one Quechuan, and the other Q'ero. Now, my actual exposure to the Q'ero has been very limited (how I ended up having a tiny old Q'ero shaman bashing me in the head with a blanket full of sacred rocks is a long story, best left for some other venue than this), and I've been interested to find out more "details" on their specific practices. A month or so back I stumbled over J.E. Williams' The Andean Codex: Adventures and Initiations Among the Peruvian Shamans[2] on Amazon, and thought it sounded interesting enough to order.

This is, however, a *very* odd little (about 200 pages) book. The author is a "doctor of Oriental and naturopathic medicine" and has been spending much of his career hanging about various Native American tribal groups investigating their healing techniques. This book would have benefited *greatly* had he also picked up an *editor* somewhere along the way! The Andean Codex[3], while *fascinating* in some of its details, varies widely in tone and focus, occasionally threatening to veer off into Newage blithering, and frequently descending to "typing up the journal" levels of mundane minutia.

The book starts off in the Amazon, with the author (and some other introduced, then dropped, characters) experiencing Ayahuasca. The jungle Shaman says that Williams has had such a powerful experience (*uh-huh*) that he *has to go to the Andes* to work it all out (???). The next chapter starts a few years later, he's returning to Peru, and is doing the necessary tourist trip up to Machu Picchu, where he runs into a "world peace" event featuring three Tibetan lamas and three Q'ero shamans. Oddly enough, nobody organizing this seems to have provided for *translation*, so he steps in to conveniently provide a Spanish-English bridge between the Shaman that conveniently speaks some Spanish and the Lama that conveniently speaks some English. Once again, characters are introduced, developed, and dropped. He ends up waiting for a train (without reservations) with the Q'ero (who conveniently *do* have tickets "but don't know what they are"), and they all eventually get back to Cuzco, and he starts working with them over the next several years. Again, the "convenience" of the various events described begs the reader's "suspension of disbelief" beyond what most books would (even of the "shamanic genre"), and generally sets one's "B.S. detectors" into full alert.

This is *not* helped by the oddest part of the book, when he does a seemingly pointless (and very "Newagey") story of when he was on a pilgrimage to Mt. Shasta back in the 70's, and "miraculously" finds the Shasta Abbey and is seen by some holy lady who has been in solitary retreat (and "doesn't see anybody" but sees *him* because she's "been waiting for him" ... *uh-huh*) who relates a story about an expedition to the fabled lost Incan city of Paititi, while naming folks that one would assume would have a function in the over-all context of the book. Again, characters and plot lines are developed and then discarded, with only the idea "looking for Paititi" (discussed with the Q'ero) resurfacing later.

Eventually, the Q'ero have him come up to their high-mountain land, and he gets terribly altitude sick and nearly dies (here is where he sounds like he's just regurgitating his journals about what hurt, what he ate/drank, how he slept, etc.). He survives, and in the last chapter returns to the Amazon. Huh? Obviously, there *is* something to be said about non-linear narratives, but the book reads more like this is due to editorial abandonment rather than stylistic intent!

Now, there *is* useful material in this book, although the "Codex" of the title can be pretty much reduced down to a handful of "ethical principles" ... these are: *munay*, "lovingkindness/beauty", *yachay*, "correct knowledge", *llank'ay*, "right action", *kawsay*, "respect for life processes", and *ayni*, "reciprocity". While spun out in various stories and examples, this hardly compromises a "codex", and this would have been a much *better* book had the intent of making "a book representing Andean spiritual life" been focused on without the other (self-congratulatory) stuff.

As this is a relatively recent (especially for my collection) release, it does still appear to be in print, so were you so inclined, you should be able to find it at your local book store, but Amazon has it discounted a third off of cover, and their new/used vendors have "new" copies for about half of that. While I was interested in this for the look at the Q'ero, you likely are not operating with that connection, as such (unless you're hot for "Newagey" fluff), it is hard for me to recommend this largely incoherent book. As noted above, this *could have been* beaten into something of substance, but it's way too self-indulgent in the broad strokes and too cursory in the details to be something I'd tell just anybody to go pick up.

Notes

1. http://btripp-books.livejournal.com/31595.html

2-3. http://amzn.to/29Vpviz

Thursday, March 15, 2007[1]

Not what you'd expect ...

Carlos Castaneda's The Wheel of Time: The Shamans of Ancient Mexico, Their Thoughts About Life, Death and the Universe[2] is a book that sort of "willed itself" into existence. Castaneda had been wanting to do some collection of the actual sayings of Don Juan, and had started to extract them from his various books. He had intended to do something of an encyclopedia of the teachings, arranged by topic, subject, etc., but found that the quotes were "too slippery" to be able to satisfactorily organize that way. However, when he read through them in chronological order, they appeared to have their own inner organization, and so he ended up just going with that. Each of the first eight books have their own chapter, with one quote per page, followed by a few pages of Castaneda putting that "phase of the teachings" into context. This makes for a fascinating presentation, something of a Yaqui Shaman's *Tao Te Ching*!

I suppose I should offer up a significant caveat, however ... I have read all of the source books from which The Wheel of Time[3] draws, so the narratives where these originally appeared are, to a greater or lesser extent, familiar to me, thus making Castaneda's commentaries on them more cogent to me than they would likely be to somebody coming to the material "cold". That said, this may very well be able to stand on its own as "a book of Yaqui wisdom" in a way that the previous book[4] I reviewed *failed* to do (despite its stated intents) for the wisdom of the Q'ero!

Now, I have been studying Shamanism for a *long time* (although I've never personally worked with any Yaqui/"Toltec" practitioners), so I have a certain set of "filters" through which the material processes. One particular quote stood out as a "universal (shamanic) truth", that I figured I'd share here ... this is from the section taken from The Eagle's Gift[5]:

> *"All the faculties, possibilities, and accomplishments of shamanism, from the simplest to the most astounding, are in the human body itself."*

This is an important point that I think gets glossed over too frequently when dealing with "comparative shamanism", how the "internal states" of shamanic practitioners, from the Arctic to the Amazon, from Tibet to Teotihuacan, all have a core "base reality" that is common despite the myriad of outer trappings of ritual, entheogens, or cultural-specific myth. This suggests to me that the "mystical plane" accessed by shamanic practitioners is somehow hard-wired into the human nervous/energetic architecture and what the world knows as "religion" is simply the hollow shells of one-time direct perceptions of the ultimate and/or divine reality, hijacked by priests, politicians, and every variation of "church ladies" to suppress and control mankind.

Anyway, with the caveat outlined above, I would recommend this book to all and sundry. It is a "book of wisdom" from a tradition that doesn't have its own surviving *historical* version, and seems to have willed itself into being ... who's gonna argue with *that*? The Wheel of Time[6] does seem to be still in print in a paperback edition (and would thereby possibly be found at your local bookstore), but "like new" copies of the hardcover (which is what I have) can be had from Amazon's new/used vendors for just over five bucks. Hey, a nice hardcover edition of a *self-generated book of wisdom*, with shipping for under $9 ... why not go for it?

Notes:

1. http://btripp-books.livejournal.com/31922.html
2-3. http://amzn.to/29Q7t0T
4. http://btripp-books.livejournal.com/31595.html
5. http://btripp-books.livejournal.com/25256.html
6. http://amzn.to/29Q7t0T

Thursday, March 22, 2007[1]

Verrrrrry Interrrresting ...

I doubt that anybody will ever really know "the truth" about Carlos Castaneda and his apprenticeship with Don Juan Matus. The settings and details of the early books have been widely challenged, and it appears that in his later years, Castaneda's life was a bit of a hall of mirrors. This is another of the "final books" which were published, if not posthumously, at least right at the time of his death. Those three books (this, *The Wheel of Time* and *Magical Passes*) were all quite different from his previous work, each approaching what has since become known as the "Toltec" tradition from a slightly different angle. In The Active Side of Infinity[2] Castaneda looks at events in his own life that had particularly intense effects on him, as part of a "warrior's album" of the struggle between the sorcerer's "two minds", the natural mind vs. *"the foreign installation"*.

The book contains a dozen or so "stories" supposedly based on events in Castaneda's life, which all lead back to the concept from the title, that of *"infinity"*, one of those typically slippery terms in his books which gets presented, but not necessarily nailed down with a "normal perception" definition. Don Juan tells him: *"Sorcerers have only one point of reference: **infinity**."*, and that he must disengage from all his mundane points of reference. The stories here are about events which brought the author (from a young lad right up through his later years) in touch with *"infinity"*. As to what this *means*, the closest that I can come (having not studied with any "Toltec" teachers) to what I believe is being meant with this is the sense of gut-twisting vertigo that one gets when, say, contemplating the expansion of the universe (or maybe that's just me).

Anyway, each chapter (which build up into various thematic sections) focuses on one story, and Don Juan's take on what realization that Castaneda should have from that. As with most of his books, there are new concepts introduced in The Active Side of Infinity[3], the most fascinating being a type of *"inorganic being"* called a "flyer" which the sorcerers "see" as a leaping shadow. These beings, according to Don Juan, attached themselves to humanity a few thousand years ago, and feed off of us (consuming parts of our energy fields, the *"glowing coat of awareness"*), creating the "normal reality" via *"the foreign installation"* to keep us controlled, something along the ways that people keep chickens in a coop. These beings were not always attached to us, and before that humans were "complete beings" and able to do various mythic/heroic things. The "flyers" can be stymied, however, via what Don Juan describes as "discipline" (a way of engaging "infinity") which ends up effecting the energies of our "glowing coat of awareness" and making that unpalatable as a food source; once they no longer are "pruning" it, this begins to grow back to its natural state (hence the seeming "amazing powers" wielded by the sorcerers).

Needless to say, "Your Mileage May Vary" when dealing with this sort of esoterica. Having at this point read pretty much all of Castaneda's books, this fits in as well as any of the "out there" concepts (like "The Eagle" consuming one's energy upon death if one hasn't learned to slip by it, as described in *The Eagle's Gift*[4]) that he's presented, so it "fits" in the over-all development of the "Toltec" mythos. I must admit, however, there were *several* points in the book where I just plain didn't believe his stories, not for over-the-top metaphysical wookie-wookie, but for (to pick one example) that he was a pool shark at age 9 or so, sneaking out of the house at night to work for professional gamblers (billiards never, to my recall, having been mentioned in any of the previous books!).

This said, it was a fairly engrossing read, and one I'd certainly recommend to anybody "into this stuff", although hardly as a starting place for those not familiar with the Castaneda material! The Active Side of Infinity[5] is in print in a paperback edition (so should be easy enough to find), although I got a "very good" (which ended up being indistinguishable from "new") copy of the hardcover for under nine bucks with shipping from the Amazon new/used vendors.

Notes:

1. http://btripp-books.livejournal.com/32216.html
2-3. http://amzn.to/29VnNOh
4. http://btripp-books.livejournal.com/25256.html
5. http://amzn.to/29VnNOh

Sunday, March 25, 2007[1]

What a shame ...

(sigh) I was sort of hoping that this was going to a book of "practical shamanism" from Castaneda (ala Serge King's fabulous *Urban Shaman*), but it's neither "practical", nor really by Castaneda. As I noted in my previous review, by the end of his life, Carlos Castaneda was living in a "hall or mirrors" where nothing was what it seemed, and it *could* be argued that this was true for his whole work, but the pretense is most blatantly obvious here.

I have *a lot* to discuss about Castaneda's work, but I'm going to try to make this review first deal with the book at hand, Magical Passes: The Practical Wisdom of the Shamans of Ancient Mexico[2], which is (essentially) a manual for the *Tensegrity* exercises that Castaneda and his inner circle began teaching in 1993 (the same time that his last "substantial" book, *The Art of Dreaming*, came out). This basically presents several hundred "moves", with photos and detailed descriptions, with section introductions that serve to explain the purpose of the "magical passes" ... except that they *don't*. This is the most frustrating aspect of this book, almost *nothing* in it is put into an actual energetic context, a scant handful of the exercises have any sort of an explanation of *why* one might be doing it, and that is typically only in the form of "moving some X energy to Y spot", without a reason that you might be seeking to do this.

As Castaneda in his other books is *always* trying to figure out WHY stuff is being done, this is a huge clue that he didn't write the bulk of this book. Now, I do believe that the introductory bits for each section *are* based on his notes, yet these are very uneven, ranging from classic Castaneda to stuff that I can't believe got past an editor (Don Juan is at one point "quoted" as saying *"friggin'"*!). Frankly, much of what's in here has no specific purpose ... parts of it seem to be "instructions from the Ministry of Silly Walks", and other parts seem like somebody trying to take the instructions for Rocky Horror's *Time Warp* and making them "sacred motions". Oddly enough, the most "Castaneda-sounding" part is the introduction to the section dealing with "passes" for *Recapitulation*, a process that in the books is generally followed in what is essentially *a box*, not exactly the ideal situation for doing gymnastics!

Now, I will admit that I have not bothered to *try* these various motions, but I have done a good deal of "energy work" over the years, and one thing that is consistent from tradition to tradition is that one is usually given rather detailed instructions of *what one is supposed to be doing with the* **energy**, however in Magical Passes[3] the closest you get to that is directions "to move like you're pulling something physical" or the like, no "why" just a whole lot of "what" which is (at best) described as "freeing up energy" or "shifting energy". As such, the book is a *hugely boring* read, with 450 pictures (a significant portion which look like step-by-step instructions for Steve Martin's "Funky Tut") and accompanying turn/pull/twist/swing/whatever directions.

As noted above, I doubt that Castaneda had very much to do with this book, as it was another that came out either right at the time of his death or posthumously. There are bits and pieces here which "sound like him", but these are rare flashes in otherwise drab prose, liberally sprinkled with bits that don't sound like him at all. Here is where I'm going to veer off into "speculation" and only deal with this book peripherally.

Now, I *do* believe that Castaneda had contact with authentic shamanic teachers, especially in the 60's and 70's, although it is hard to argue with those who insist that much of what he presents as Don Juan's teachings seem to come from various "old world" traditions (be they Western or Eastern). In any case, I think that Castaneda had gotten his "authentic teachings" in over the course of his "classic" first five books. At that point it seems like he disengaged from whatever teachers that he had been working with and returned to Los Angeles and set himself up as some sort of a "guru", pulling in the various women that were to suddenly appear in the later stories. There is a fascinating site out there called Sustained Action[4], which was set up by former students of Castaneda to "try to make sense" of the various twisty bits of myth-making surrounding his teaching, and much of what follows is drawn from the things that I found there.

It is my belief that Magical Passes[5] is a book done *by* Florinda Donner-Grau, Taisha Abelar and possibly Carol Tiggs and others to "push" their *Tensegrity* exercises as Castaneda faded. As early as 1974, Florinda and Taisha were "a team", being featured in a martial arts magazine demonstrating assorted Karate moves. If anything, the exercises resemble something more like Tai Chi (but without any sense of actual *chi*!) than anything that I've ever seen a Shaman perform (although I have had teachers who have been very adamant that any "action" requires a physical component, but this can be as subtle as a little flick of a finger, and not an entire system of "dramatic" motions). Again, I highly recommend the Sustained Action[6] site for some amazing research into chronologies, etc. for the women that Castaneda pulled in around him. Most of these figure prominently in his later books, although it appears that none were where they were supposed to have been in them. Castaneda seems to have had a strange paranoia about images and names, forbidding his inner circle to be photographed, and having them frequently legally changing their names (often with several using the same "legal address" to do so, which could then be conveniently abandoned). They also seemed to get married and divorced a lot ... and not just in a "L.A." sense, but having marriages come and go over a 3-week period.

One of the clues that this system was created by "the Witches" (as they were called) is that one whole section of these exercises were "specific" to each of Castaneda's women ... which is all well and good except that these are supposed to be *ancient* forms! I suppose that if one says that Taisha Abelar is *the stalker*, Florinda Donner-Grau is *the dreamer*, Carol Tiggs is *the nagual woman*, and The Blue Scout, is, well, *a scout*, then they're simply in the role of *archetypes*, but I suspect not.

Interestingly, all these women have disappeared. Of course, with all the name, spouse, and address changing they did, they might very well be out there somewhere "under the radar", but following Castaneda's death (April 27, 1998 though not publicly announced until June) they dropped out of sight, although still supposedly "directing" the Tensegrity programs of Castaneda's Cleargreeen organization. In 2003 the desiccated (and coyote-disturbed) bones of "The Blue Scout" were found in Death Valley, and some believe that all of Castaneda's women committed suicide in an effort to follow him (despite his dying a rather mundane, nasty, death from liver cancer instead of "burning from within" and "sneaking past The Eagle" as Don Juan and his party supposedly did). Of course, there had been books by Taisha Abelar (*The Sorcerer's Crossing*, among others) and Florinda Donner-Grau (the less-than-stellar *Shabono*), but nothing since Castaneda's death.

Anyway ... as anybody who had read this far no doubt suspects, I can't recommend Magical Passes[7] unless you're getting it just to complete your Castaneda collection. I don't think it's really by him. I don't think that it has anything to do with Shamanic knowledge. I do know that it's got about 30 pages of worthwhile stuff, while the other 200 pages are just crap. If you do feel a need of adding this to your library, it's still in print in paperback, but you could pick up a "like new" hardcover for under five bucks via the Amazon new/used vendors. Again, this ain't gonna add much to anybody's knowledge about anything, but sometimes you just gotta have it on the shelf.

Notes:

1. http://btripp-books.livejournal.com/32339.html
2-3. http://amzn.to/2a5deuc
4. http://www.sustainedaction.org/
5. http://amzn.to/2a5deuc
6. http://www.sustainedaction.org/
7. http://amzn.to/2a5deuc

Friday, April 6, 2007[1]

If you want a Shamanic book ...

I'm usually up front with it when I'm in a position to not be particularly objective about a book, but this one is a double-whammy in that regard. Not only have I traveled and studied with Alberto Villoldo frequently over the past quarter century, but Alberto even floated the concept about my possibly co-authoring "a book on soul retrieval" with him back in 1996. Frankly, I'm amazed that it took him so long to get this out (in 2005), as he seemed to be thinking of this as a "next project" back then. Interestingly (and in sharp contrast to his earlier books), there does not seem to be a co-author involved in Mending The Past And Healing The Future with Soul Retrieval[2], so this seems to be Alberto on his own.

One of the problems I have in dealing with Alberto's books is that, in some of the early instances, I was *there* for specific events, and they rarely played out on the page the way things had been on the ground. I subsequently found (from Alberto) that his "technique" for "writing" his early books was to assemble all his field notes into a file box and drop it off for his co-author to make some narrative sense of. Not unlike Castaneda, there is a "haziness" of the particulars surrounding the teachings (I recall one time Alberto talking about *burning his journals*, which totally freaked me out, only to find similar-sounding journals "referenced" in this book!). A startling example of this in Soul Retrieval[3] is referring to his teachers as the *Laika* ... which seems to be an amalgam of his original Quechuan teachers (Don Eduardo Calderon primarily), and his later work with the Q'ero. *Why* fictionalize the name? And *why* pick the name of the dog that the USSR sent to its death in space on Sputnik 2? I'm still trying to figure *that* one out!

All that being said, Soul Retrieval[4] is quite a good book. Alberto spins out the soul retrieval "process" bit by bit through the chapters, focusing on one thing (and, typically, one "meditation") at a time, but these are woven through with literary allusions (he uses the story of Parsifal extensively, as well as various Biblical snippets such as David & Goliath) and "case studies" from his own consulting practice. Now, having *done* (earlier) permutations of this work with him, I had several points in the book where I was thinking "Wait, why aren't we doing *this* now?" or "Huh? What's up with doing *that* there?" I also felt that at some points he was glossing over material that had featured significantly in various trainings that I'd been through, but I'm aware that this could simply be MY perspective and that the stuff in question is perhaps not as essential to Alberto's current model of soul retrieval. There was a point towards the end of the book, however, that I felt he (or his editor) had made a decision to "abbreviate" the process, as the established "flow" of the book switches and a number of particular exercises are described, but not walked through in detail. As a former editor/publisher I could see the "detailed version" being eyed warily as being "too repetitive", but the resulting parts of the book seem to be "glossed over" rather than fully presented.

Despite its subject (and a few ventures "into the light", as it were) Alberto Villoldo's Soul Retrieval[5] is *delightfully* "non-newagey", having the feel of a training manual mixed with "clinical" observations, journal notations, etc., and tied together with literary allusions ... a combination that was quite a nice change from my other recent reading! Being a fairly recent release, this is available both in hardcover and paperback, so you should be able to find it in your local store, although I snagged a "like new" copy of the hardback via the Amazon new/used vendors. If you have an interest in this particular Shamanic practice, this is a good one to pick up!

Notes:

1. http://btripp-books.livejournal.com/32742.html
2-5. http://amzn.to/29F8PNe

Sunday, April 8, 2007[1]

(sigh)

I was highly disappointed in this book. As those of you "keeping score" will recall, last fall I completed a course resulting in my being a "Certified Hypnotist", and I've been trying to take some "baby steps" towards actually developing some sort of a "consulting" practice. I'd been looking for some "practical" manual for setting up something along those lines, and Shelley Stockwell's Hypnosis: How to Put a Smile on Your Face and Money in Your Pocket[2] appeared to be specifically addressing this. Sadly, not only was this *not* generally the case, but 90% of this book is the sort of New Age twaddle that I would think *most* Hypnotists would be mortified at being associated with.

It appears that somewhere along the line, Ms. Stockwell obtained a Ph.D., which perhaps lured me into thinking "how bad can it be?", but I was really unprepared for just *how bad* it was. The "Stockwell System" is based in that "airy-fairy" mindset that gives all of California, much of Oregon and Washington, and large chunks of New Mexico such a bad name. The book is *filled* with bits of bad "cutesy" poetry, *really bad* "pun" mis-spellings of things ("abundance" is, for example, frequently stretched out as *"a bun dance"*), and the authors' assorted vacation pictures (with nothing to do with the text, but I guess they're there for the IRS) and silly drawings. What's worse (speaking as a former publisher), there are what I assume to be *unintentional* misspellings (and various typographical errors) all through the text, in some areas as frequent as one per 3-4 pages, which suggests that this nearly-500 page spewing (counting the couple of dozen pages of ads for her books, tapes, and classes in the back) was "home set" by the author on her Mac and not bothered to be proofread.

Strangely enough, this book starts out as if the reader had never encountered Hypnosis previously, and spends maybe half its length as a basic primer. There is a particular horror involved in imagining the sort of mush-brained NewAger who picks up this book, sets it to memory, and hangs a shingle out as a therapist. Unfortunately, that scenario could go a long way to explaining a lot of quirks of California, etc. While Stockwell does cover a lot of *stuff*, it's all presented in the worst possible "touchy-feely" mode, piling fluff-bunny cliché on top of fluff-bunny cliché, resulting in having precious little in it useful for a "serious" practitioner. I had *hoped* to have been able to at least extract some "templates" from this, but except for a snippet here and there, it's all so bogged down in delusional thinking that the "translation" does not seem to be worth the effort.

Now, this is not to say that there is *nothing* of use in this book, only that the subset of what I had bought the book for, and what is actually in the book, would be about a 24-page pamphlet! Of course, this *is* from my perspective. If your worldview leans towards believing that you were an Aztec princess in direct communication with UFO intelligences in a previous life, and you demand that every little thing in your paisley pony world coddles your delusions like they were packed in ethereal cotton candy, I'm sure that you'd *love* this manual. Depressingly, this is still in print (not surprising, I guess, being that it's produced by Stockwell's own "Creativity Unlimited" press), so is being actively foisted on an unsuspecting public, and it can be had for about half price used via the usual vendors, but even that's too much to pay for this "newage spewage" (I, fortunately, got a copy for only $3.25 before shipping, so my disgust is tempered by frugality). Seriously, if you're not a "hearts & unicorns" type, don't bother.

Notes:

1. http://btripp-books.livejournal.com/32954.html
2. http://amzn.to/29Ob8Ml

Monday, April 16, 2007[1]

A very worthwhile read ...

I frequently wonder why some books (which are not, on their surface, "popular" types) end up being held by so many folks. Of course, my data from this largely comes from LibraryThing[2], so is from a self-selecting subset of book readers, but I *notice* (as it effects my collection's "obscurity rating") when a book is listed by a lot of other users there ... in this case 864 (whereas a substantial chunk of my recently-read books are shared by 0-10 others!). My usual supposition, in cases where this would be plausible, is that said book has been used as a textbook, and found its way into a lot of people's libraries due to being *assigned* rather than sought out.

I would like to *think* that a large number of people ran out to buy Carl Sagan's The Demon-Haunted World: Science as a Candle in the Dark[3] for its content, but I'm not that hopeful about the intellect of humanity. Sagan's book is, at its core, a long lament about how our culture has lost its grounding in science and has slid into a rather dire illiteracy on the subject. However, it is not *structured* this way, rather being a series of broadsides at a wide variety of non-scientific "belief systems".

Frankly, as I read The Demon-Haunted World[4], I was quite enthusiastic about the book and kept thinking of various friends to whom I would very much recommend this; however, there was at least *something* in here which would prove to be extremely offensive to nearly *every* person that popped up on my mental list, some trashing of a particular "sacred cow" that was enough that I was not willing to be "the messenger" who was likely to be the focus of the ire of a wounded paradigm.

After a couple of introductory chapters framing the importance of science, Sagan starts (unsurprisingly) with looking at "The Face on Mars" and similar things, and how they are promoted by the likes of Hoagland (pointedly not mentioned by name) to the Weekly World News. From there he looks at Alien abductions, UFOs, hallucinations, religious visions, "ritual abuse", ghosts, and various questionable therapies such as "repressed memory" and "past life regression", spinning an interesting matrix in which these all seem to be manifestations of a single underlying psychological and/or mental dysfunction. He then looks at how most delusions are propagated (his postulate that there is an invisible fire-breathing dragon in his garage, and how he can generate excuses why any *test* to actually prove or disprove the existence of said dragon can be parried in exactly the same way that most paranormal claimants brush off any attempts to test the realities of their pet postulates) and something of the mind-set of those devoted to the unprovable.

The last third or so of the book goes into more societal issues, looking at ways that the lack of scientific knowledge (or the impact of "anti-scientific" thinking) has decayed the base of our civilization, from how we know things to how we govern. Again, nearly everybody has a sacred cow gored here ...

it's not just the tens of thousands of fluff-bunny newagers who are *certain* they were Cleopatra in a previous life, but right-wingers who would gladly budget for "one more Blackhawk helicopter" but bluster about the "waste" of spending the same dollars on a "pure science" project. He has a particularly chilling look at Christianity, especially as it relates to the abuses of the "Witch trials" of the 15th through 18th centuries, and how "insular" belief systems can spawn the most inhuman abuses, and how similar sorts of patterns crop up whenever there isn't a "rational counterpoint" to balance faith, nationalism, etc.. My own buttons got pushed a bit in his analysis of how poorly our current "conservative" politicians (who are certainly more sane than their leftist counterparts) compare to America's "Founding Fathers", who were very strongly supportive of the "scientific paradigm" as seen by the philosophers of The Enlightenment (many of whom, like Jefferson, were both).

While I don't think there are many people who would not be made *uncomfortable* reading one section or another of Sagan's The Demon-Haunted World[5], I do highly recommend it to all and sundry. I suppose that it would be too much to ask that it be included in the basic High School curriculum (after all, this is written at something higher than a fifth-grade comprehension level), it should definitely be one of those books *strongly suggested*. I, myself, walked away from this with some *practical* realizations of what to steer clear of in doing hypnosis, and there are many "points of clarity" that would benefit anybody reading it. This is (thankfully) still in print, and Amazon has the paperback *new* for just over ten bucks, with used copies going for as little as three bucks. Go get a copy!

Notes:

1. http://btripp-books.livejournal.com/33163.html
2. http://btripp-books.com/
3-5. http://amzn.to/29Oasql

Thursday, April 19, 2007[1]

A really good book ...

Every now and again I run across a book which is a perfect fit for a "need" I've had, and Brooke Allen's Moral Minority: Our Skeptical Founding Fathers[2] is one of these. Over the years I have had some knock-down-drag-out on-line arguments with assorted Xtian fundamentalists who have been trying to "sell" the notion that the U.S.A. is a "Christian Nation" ... to which my response has been that they are either blatant *liars*, knowing that this is not the case, yet promoting the falsehood willingly, or absolute *morons* that have no idea of the history/personalities involved! It would appear that Ms. Allen has had some similar run-ins with the Fundies in her past, as this book is clearly intended to shed some light on the subject.

Now, it obviously is *true* that many of the initial English groups making the journey over to settle in The New World *were* various sorts of religious fanatics (my own ancestors on the Mayflower being possible examples), who were simply looking for a place where they could practice their particular *brand* of lunacy, unfettered by the official "loyalty tests" (for one favored sect or another) present in nearly all countries in The Old World. However, these initial settlements have more in common with the Guyana suicide-cult of Jonestown than they do with the founding of the United States.

The concept of America, and its governance, came from minds deeply steeped in the Enlightenment, Deists, Masons, Unitarians, and the like. Yes, there *were* partisans of various sects (most of the Protestant churches were mutually quite hostile, and constantly jostling for governmental influence) involved in the Revolution and represented among the leadership of the new nation, but these were, by and large, not the *main players*. Moral Minority[3] takes a look at six of "the leading lights", Franklin, Washington, Adams, Jefferson, Madison, and Hamilton, along with some key supporting documents (as well as fascinating references to source materials). Lest the theocracy fans say "well, maybe those six were an aberration" (despite including our first four Presidents), the author only peripherally touches on the *extreme* "anti-Christians" involved in the Revolution and the Founding, men like Thomas Paine, Ethan Allan, and assorted followers of the atheistic Hume, the barely deistic Voltaire (a close friend of both Franklin and Jefferson) and the other intellectual leaders of the Enlightenment in Europe.

Unfortunately, the Fundamentalists these days have the woeful state of American education as an ally. Just as Carl Sagan was lamenting the lack of *scientific* literacy in the previous book[4] reviewed here (also leading to some of the bi-polar newage/fundy idiocy in our culture), a sub-text to Allen's book could be the near total lack of historical literacy in the USA. I doubt that two of ten people stopped on the street would be able to give a "thumbnail" description of the Enlightenment, let alone naming its major figures. Is it any wonder that the Xtian theocrats are able to blatantly claim that English common law has a Christian basis, when it dates back *at least* to Queen Martia (and the book of "Martian Law" ... no relation to Valentine

Michael Smith's dictates, I'm sure) in the mid-4th Century **B.C.E.**? Needless to say, I wish that this book could become a "social studies" classroom standard!

As much as I like Moral Minority[5], I do have some caveats. The first is that, when finished, I felt like I wished the book had been half again as long, and covering much more of the "source material" which inspired the Founders. Yes, this is well referenced in the notes (and I have sought out a number of these texts), and it would have, perhaps, watered down the impact of the book as being *about* these six men, but I still felt like I "wanted more". The second caveat is that I believe that the author does herself a disservice (in a book that could well be a resource for decades of readers) in taking little pot-shots at George Bush (5 or 6 times) and Ronald Reagan (at least once). In most cases, these aren't even part of substantive arguments (for which the "Christian" bent of the current conservative movement could certainly provide valid talking points), but casually dropped barbs. Even today, these give the text a "dated" feel, and I really wish her editor had excised those before allowing the book to go to press.

That being said, I *highly recommend* picking up a copy of Moral Minority[6], either as ammunition in the fight against religious fundamentalism, or to open one's eyes to the *deeply* secular intent of our Founding Fathers. As this is a new book, you can no doubt find it at your local bookstore, but Amazon has the hardcover at nearly ten bucks off of cover price. This is *definitely* one that everybody should read!

Notes:

1. http://btripp-books.livejournal.com/33522.html

2-3. http://amzn.to/2a1VW0Y

4. http://btripp-books.livejournal.com/33163.html

5-6 http://amzn.to/2a1VW0Y

Friday, April 27, 2007[1]

Clap your hands if you believe ...

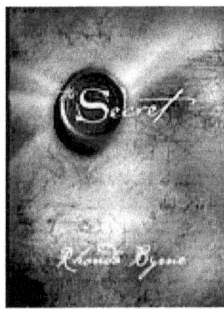

Ah, poor Tinkerbell ... I'm afraid that if it came down to me, she'd have been toast. And, that's the key problem I had with this book. Now, those of you who follow my reading via these reviews (or my main journal) are asking yourself *"What the heck is Brendan doing reading something from Oprah's list?"*, and I've had to ask myself that several times as well while working through this one. If, however, you *are* a regular reader, you'll recall that I have been in a long, frustrating, and seemingly futile search for paying employment over the past ... well, lets just say *very long time*. I was venting about this situation at a close family friend's wake (yeah, I know), and an acquaintance that I hadn't seen for the better part of 30 years was *fervent* in her recommendation of Rhonda Byrne's book The Secret[2], and I'm just desperate enough that I figured it was as good a use of my time as cranking out another hundred resumes that will be summarily round-filed by assorted HR drones.

Of course, The Secret[3] is exactly the sort of book that I would, in the normal flow of events, simply mock. However, having had at least a second-hand rave presented to me as to its usefulness (the gal knew this elderly couple who were even in a worse hole that we are and who managed to "use this" to change everything around in a matter of months), I dove in. Now, this is not a *bad* book, and has a reasonably interesting structure, being built around blurbs by assorted "new age success guru" types, and interspersed with quotes from sources ranging from the Bible and Buddha to Winston Churchill and Albert Einstein, all of which *do* seem to be pointing to the same "secret". As I was telling a newage bookstore owner a couple of days ago, these "references" *did* manage to keep my "BS meter" in check while reading this.

So, you're itching to know "The Secret", right? OK .. here ya go: "You need to feel good and *really believe* that you already have whatever it is you're focusing on" ... that being a bit condensed and paraphrased, but the essential thrust of the book. Sounds just *ducky*, doesn't it? Why, I'll go right out and write all those checks that I've been holding off on because ... because ... because ... oh, *DRAT!*, the reality of my checking account balance just intruded and *ruined everything*! I guess I don't have "perfect belief" (and I now feel like crap).

And there be the rub ... or rubs, actually. See, first of all, this stuff doesn't work unless you are a Happy Shiny People type ... depressed? sad? stressed? angsty? ... well, too bad for *you*, Mr. Pouty-Face ... no Unlimited Abundance from the Universe *for you!* ... no, you have to "snap out of it" and be HAPPY! Now, if anybody reading this has ever had to deal with depression, how *useful* was it to be told (not that the book puts it in *those words*, but that's the essence) to "snap out of it"? Not very, right? In fact, that approach is pretty much *counter-productive* from what I've ever seen/heard/experienced. But, "The Secret" doesn't work unless "you turn that frown upside down!".

OK, so, just for argument's sake, say that your "staring into the abyss" sort of guy manages to painfully wrest some twisted facsimile of a smile (ala Christina Ricci's brilliant portrayal of Wednesday Adams) out of the deep morose depths of his IRL existence, what then? Ah ... *believing* that what you want is already yours, and *acting* like what you want is already yours. Now, I'm not angling for *a car*, I'm not angling for *a house*, I'm trying to get *a job* that I wouldn't hate, or, better yet, a huge sum of money (they say the "how" doesn't matter, and that it is "as easy" to manifest a million dollars as a single dollar, so I picked a *hundred million dollars* as nice round figure) to manifest. What am I supposed to *do*, show up at some random office at 8:30am and plop myself down in an empty cubicle? Start kiting checks as in the above? What? Well, obviously, I don't have good enough "belief".

And that's the second real ball-buster about "The Secret" ... if you don't believe well enough, not only will Tinkerbell *die*, but you won't get the goodies. This reminds me of Xtian fundamentalists who suddenly turn on their own when they're found with gay hookers or a briefcase full of blow ... "they weren't *real* Christians!" is the typical cop-out. Well, just as how the fundies cut-and-run from any "Christian" who has the bad luck to *get caught*, it seems like "The Secret" only works for those who clap real hard and chant that they believe. If you *don't* get the stuff your heart desires, well, *sorry, Skippy*, I guess you should have wiped the prints off the steering wheel when you took that unscheduled test drive of the BMW.

Oddly enough, I didn't *hate* this book. It's well enough written, has interesting stuff from interesting people, is quite attractively designed, and avoids being newage treacle for the most part ... it's just that the *logic* of it seems to be lacking, and that only like 1/10th of 1% of the people reading this would be able to do the mental gyrations to not only deny the factual realities of their current existence enough to generate the necessary internal emotional state for this "to work", *and* walk the tight-rope between a delusional level of belief in *having something they don't* and getting thrown in jail for acting on that delusion! This has, of course, practically become a cult, with videos, audios, and a web site (where you can download "blank checks" from the "Universal Bank (Un)Limited" to better visualize money manifesting), so a lot of folks are no doubt buying into it.

Maybe I'm too far down towards the Pits of Hell for this stuff to be any good for me ... if *you* want to have a go at The Secret[4], you can barely walk past a bookstore without getting hit over the head with it. Amazon has it for 40% off of cover, but the new/used guys are asking almost that, so you're looking at discounted retail on this one. Again, it wasn't a *bad book* just something that seems to have too damn many caveats to really get me on board.

Notes:

1. http://btripp-books.livejournal.com/33791.html

2-4. http://amzn.to/1mOgxao

Tuesday, May 1, 2007[1]

Another decent one ...

I'm always so *happy* when I launch into a "newage" book (for whatever reason) and find it not "silly", and this is another of those pleasantly-surprising volumes!

I ended up ordering this from Amazon the same time as *The Secret*[2] as they both were about a wash on the discount rate vs. the new/used rate plus shipping, and together I could get them new and with free shipping, so they're sort of linked in my mind because of that. I actually got turned on to this via a gal at my Toastmasters club, who had done a speech about it a month or so back.

Frankly, don Miguel Ruiz' The Four Agreements: A Practical Guide to Personal Freedom, A Toltec Wisdom Book[3] could hardly be more different, especially in that it doesn't demand *belief*, just personal effort, which, while *difficult* is certainly within the grasp of anybody. Likewise, it does not depend on any supernatural agencies, just what one as a normal person can muster on a daily basis.

Now, as I have mentioned previously, I have read pretty much all of the "Castaneda material", but very little of the post-Castaneda "Toltec" teachings. If this is a solid representation of the latter, I'm quite impressed. According to his bio, don Miguel Ruiz, is a "hereditary" shaman (both his mother and grandfather were practitioners of the local Mexican traditions), but evidently a "hesitant" one. Rather than immerse himself in his family's healing traditions, he went off to medical school and became a surgeon ... however, a near-death experience in a car crash in his 20's drew his attention back to the traditional knowledge.

While not appearing to have worked at all with Castaneda, The Four Agreements[4] shares the occasional "technical" term, but almost in passing in most instances (his definition of "allies", for instance). However, the concept of "dreaming" is central to this book, although it's not specifically like in the "dreaming/stalking" dichotomy of Castaneda, and is almost more akin to Gurdjieff's sense of "sleep". In this, he posits that all humans are "domesticated" into *"the dream of the planet"* which is the combination of the billions of individual "dreams", and is, ultimately, very much like Hell. The purpose of working with the Four Agreements is to gradually extricate oneself from the specific "agreements" which are part of that "dream" and forge a new "dream" which represents personal freedom, and ultimately "heaven on earth".

Now, the use of "agreements" is a bit confusing, as every point of acceding to the reality of the common dream is an "agreement", the Four of the title are more "rules of conduct" that will lead one to systematically address these various smaller agreements. These four steps, or "Four Agreements" are:

1. Be Impeccable With Your Word.
2. Don't Take Anything Personally.
3. Don't Make Assumptions.
4. Always Do Your Best.

The last of these is very key, because making all these "little changes" provides one with a whole bunch of opportunities for short-term failure, and it's set up this way so that one is not constantly beating oneself up for imperfection (as opposed to the "perfect belief" needed in *The Secret*!).

As one moves through one's "agreements" with the common dream, changing them over to "agreements" in line with one's personal dream, one will encounter "the parasite", a sort of extraneous consciousness which expresses itself as "The Judge" and "The Victim", alternatingly repeatedly punishing us for long-past failures ("I should not have yelled at that person", I'm bad, I'm bad, I'm bad, etc.) way past any "just" punishment, and causing us to cling to old wounds and not allow them to heal. Interestingly, the concept of our being "domesticated" into the dream, and having "the parasite" to deal with seems very close to Castaneda's "the fliers" as described in <u>The Active Side of Infinity</u>[5].

There are other "technical" terms which appear in Castaneda's books, like "attention", "warriors", and approaches to "death", and these, along with different sorts of "dreaming" lead one away from the Hell of the common dream and into the "heaven" of freely living, but the concepts are a bit too specific for me to get into at length here.

Suffice it to say that I really liked <u>The Four Agreements</u>[6], and, frankly, wished it was more in-depth than allowed by its brief 150 pages! This is still in print in both hardcover and paperback, and can be had for as little as $2.45 (plus shipping) for a "very good" used copy of the latter. However, Amazon has the hardcover for only a bit over $11.00, so I'd say *splurge* on this one, as you'll very likely find yourself wanting to re-read this, so the fancier format (with a nice silk ribbon bookmark sewn in) is worth the extra bucks (especially if you get free shipping). It should, of course, also be available via your local brick-and-mortar store. However, *do* go pick up a copy, as this is a real gem!

Notes:

1. http://btripp-books.livejournal.com/33869.html
2. http://btripp-books.livejournal.com/33791.html
3-4. http://amzn.to/29MAGXb
5. http://btripp-books.livejournal.com/32216.html
6. http://amzn.to/29MAGXb

Friday, May 4, 2007[1]

How odd ...

Yes, those of you paying attention to the parade of books here may have noticed that I've been beating myself over the head with "positive thinking" and "attracting abundance" kind of books of late, because, well, I've been in a job search for *way too long* and figure that what I've been doing *ain't working* and at this point I'd give nearly *anything* a shot, even (shudder) "positivity".

Since I *was* on this particular streak, I decided I'd throw Sanaya Roman & Duane Packer's Creating Money: Keys to Abundance[2] into the mix. Now, I've had this sitting around for nearly *six years*, having been recommended to me by Ana Voog[3] way back in 2001 (when the writing was on the wall as far as the viability of my old publishing company, and I was *starting* to look for a new gig). While I'd bought the book back then (and read a chapter or two into it), this was *not* what I was looking for at that point in time, and so ended up in a nearly-buried stack of stuff that I was "sort of reading". However, since I've been doing stuff like The Secret[4] and The Four Agreements[5] of late, this seemed to be a natural addition to the current reading line-up.

One of the things that I'd forgotten about Creating Money[6] was that it was a *channeled* book, handed down by Roman & Packer's "spirit guides" Orin and DaBen ... and, frankly, I typically have way too much cynicism to take any "channeled" book seriously, but this one surprised me. I mean, how atypical for a "newage" tome is it to have this sort of caveat:

> *"Inner guidance directs you to your higher good.*
> *Learning to distinguish inner guidance from wishful*
> *or fearful thinking is one of your challenges."*

Amazingly, this book is far more "hard edged" than a lot of "career" books I've gone through (although haven't included in my library or reviewed) of late, with many points where one might expect some gooshy newage platitude only to find these "spirit guides" telling the reader to take a long hard look at what talents, personality traits, and willingness to work they're bringing to the table!

Of course, this book is, at heart, a "look inside for your Higher Purpose" sort of thing, with meditation exercises, etc., each chapter has worksheets (OK, they're actually called "playsheets") to lead the reader to pick through their situation to figure out where they should be heading with their search. Personally, I'm not a great fan of these things, but the ones in Creating Money[7] are no worse than those in any dozen "professional" job quest books, and these frequently "cut to the chase" more that a lot of those.

Now, I have a pretty good fix on the "higher purpose" and "concrete goals" sorts of things (after six years of this crap), so a lot of where the book was leading, I'd already been; but for folks (and I've shared this with a couple of folks down at the CTC[8] who were making "career changes" and were very *eager* to do some of this sort of self-analysis) trying to figure out what they want to do with themselves, this is a good resource. Structurally, the book is set up in four main sections, "Creating Money", "Developing Mastery", "Creating Your Life's Work", and "Having Money", with several chapters to each, pretty much all with self-reflection exercises attached. There are also many dozens of "affirmations" spread through the book, which they recommend that you randomly flip through to read, although these are also themed to the particular material of the chapters in which they appear.

Oddly enough, this *does* appear to still be in print (in an edition that came out 15 years ago), so you should be able to get a copy from your local bookseller, but it can be had "used" as well through the usual suspects. If you're looking at a job transition, or just trying to get yourself "attuned for abundance", this is not a bad book to work with ... almost *despite* having been "channeled" by the authors' "spirit guides".

Notes:

1. http://btripp-books.livejournal.com/34070.html
2. http://amzn.to/2aI9VLi
3. http://anacam.com/
4. http://btripp-books.livejournal.com/33791.html
5. http://btripp-books.livejournal.com/33869.html
6-7. http://amzn.to/2aI9VLi
8. http://www.ctcchicago.org

Sunday, May 13, 2007

Maybe I just don't "get it" ...

Eckhart Tolle's The Power of Now: A Guide to Spiritual Enlightenment came *very* highly recommended to me from people who, I think, should have a better "fix" on things. Once again, this is not a "bad" book, but it's a bit of an odd duck. Of course, warning flags go up when I see something subtitled *"A Guide to Spiritual Enlightenment"*, but that's just me, I guess. Perhaps I'm less impressed with the genesis of this book than many others have been. Tolle, it appears, was a pretty "normal" guy, full of anxiety and in and out of near-suicidal depressions (OK, so my version of "normal" may not be everybody's!), who, in his late 20's had pretty much a total break-down (sounds familiar). Anyway, rather than a typical spiral down into substance abuse, Tolle had a "splitting" of his mind from his "essential being", somehow detaching from the former and finding himself living in the latter. Of course, as is usually true in breakdowns, this did not create a particularly good situation, and Tolle spent a couple of years unable to work, homeless, and spending all day sitting on park benches going "WOW!" as he looked at the world through eyes not being filtered by the mind/ego. Somehow he transitioned from "crazy guy on the park bench" to "seminar leader" (the book is rather hazy on how *that* happened), and had a new career telling people about living in a timeless "now" state. Also sketchy is Tolle's "background" ... some have talked of his "synthesis" of "ancient teachings" but his most frequently referenced work is *A Course In Miracles*, for whatever that's worth.

Now, I certainly did find many things in The Power of Now *interesting*, but there was stuff about it that just kept me scratching my head. Much of the book bounces off of "questions" that he wrote as being "typical" of the sort of things that he fields on a regular basis. One would *think* that these would come from an "academic" or "skeptical" standpoint, from which he could best defend/explain what he's trying to convey ... however, the general tone of these questions is so over-the-top "newagey" and his response frequently so *hostile* (I was, frankly, reminded of the classic Saturday Night Live skit with Jane Curtin and Dan Akroyd in a point-counterpoint take-off where Akroyd would start his rebuttal with *"Jane, you ignorant slut!"*) that you have to wonder what Tolle was "working through" in trying to turn his workshops into a book!

Tolle introduces several "concepts" of inner states, or levels of being, with varying degrees of clarity and focus. There is the concept of "psychological time" which is fairly well argued, in that the mind/ego maintains a past and projects a future in order to bolster itself, when the actual "being" is in a non-chronological "now" which does not allow for the ego construct. There is the concept of the "pain body" which is made up of wounds, physical and psychic, and exists as an independent energy entity, that can be "woken up" (think of somebody "pushing your buttons", from where does the sudden anger or hurt arise?) if one is not living in "the now". There is also "the inner body" which seems to be something like an energetic template, which brought to mind Castaneda's "the Mold of Man" (from *The Fire From Within*[4]) and even David Darling's unsettling *Zen Physics*[5] material, relating to the ultimate nature of individual/species manifestations and consciousness.

Ultimately, Tolle seems to believe that we must evolve towards this "now" state, leaving behind "temporal consciousness" and individual ego structures in favor of ... well, the specifics of his "what" are still a bit vague to me. Where Tolle *seems* to want to go reminds me of Arthur C. Clark's classic scifi book, *Childhood's End*[6] where all of humanity "evolves" into a sort of "hive mind" on its way to eventually merging with a universal "Overmind". While the state of "now" seems very much akin to a Zen satori, there is precious little in this book about *how* to get there (although a lot of what *not* to be or do), or what to *do* once one is *able* to "be in the Now". Obviously, Tolle's own *personal* response to "his enlightenment" leaves much to be desired (the above-mentioned homeless bench bliss!), and there isn't really much sense of the mundane practicality of the Zen concept of "chop wood, carry water"[7] in this. He repeatedly mentions "surrender", defined as almost a Taoistic concept of "going with the flow" rather than resisting one's life situations, but this still seems to only point towards a world filled with blissed-out glassy-eyed staring "in the Now" people, balanced both on the esoteric edge of "the end of time", and the exoteric park bench. Unfortunately, any question of "what then?" is destined to be brushed off as only being some sort of "ego ploy".

Perhaps I'm being overly hard on *The Power of Now*[8] due to it having been so "over-sold" to me and my having rather high expectations for it which it came no where near to meeting. I also wonder if this "plays better" to people less well read in the over-all "consciousness" genre, who would find things that seem easily referenced to me "remarkable insights" and great revelations. Frankly, the "now" state he describes sounds *exactly* like one I encountered back in *my* late 20's, but I guess I missed the boat by not dropping out of "mundane existence" to become a homeless prophet! Anyway, while this is still in print in *both* hardcover and paperback (and so would be likely to be found at your local bookstore), the Amazon new/used vendors have "like new" copies for as little as two bucks (plus shipping), and I'd say picking this up for cheap is better that investing retail for it.

Notes:

1. http://btripp-books.livejournal.com/34364.html
2-3. http://amzn.to/1RAvyu2
4. http://btripp-books.livejournal.com/25515.html
5. http://btripp-books.livejournal.com/7525.html
6. http://en.wikipedia.org/wiki/Childhood%27s_End
7. http://www.interluderetreat.com/meditate/chop.htm
8. http://amzn.to/1RAvyu2

Sunday, May 20, 2007[1]

A mixed bag ...

I picked this up on one of my Amazon shopping expeditions earlier this year, and, frankly, I'm not sure exactly what triggered my purchase, except the I might have just "been in a mood" to get some more Vine Deloria, Jr. in my library. Deloria is one of the major modern voices of the Native American rights movement, and has penned some really remarkable books over the years (such as God Is Red[2], reviewed here a few years back). I was saddened to find that he had passed away back in 2005, as he was a very substantial American writer.

This volume, Spirit & Reason: The Vine Deloria, Jr., Reader[3] is not, however, his best work. Rather, this is a collection of bits and pieces on various topics, some being excerpts from his various (a dozen plus editorial projects) books, others being articles originally published in assorted magazines and journals, and suffers from the realities of that structure. Also, Deloria is most powerful when writing about subjects like religion, politics, and historical realities. While these subjects are *included* in Spirit & Reason[4], they are intermixed with other materials that one feels are *not* his strong suit.

I will admit that *some* of the parts that I felt were "stretching" could have just been my own reaction to points of view that I find based on highly unlikely premises (such as the suggestion that certain types of dinosaurs were co-existing with native tribes in North America within historical times), but that could simply be my inability to detach from particular archaeological or anthropological orthodoxies. There were also some bits where I had the reaction that he was over-stating certain elements for the specific audience for which a given article was initially written, but those could likewise be simply my biases conflicting with his reality.

The book is structured in five "thematic" segments, Philosophy, Social Science, Education, Indians, and Religion, with a good deal of variety of subjects within each of these. Again, the "quality" rises and falls chapter to chapter, but that is to be expected in a collection of this nature. Personally, I would not *recommend* this for an introduction to Deloria, but would suggest if one has not read him, to start with *God Is Red*, which is a remarkable book.

This does still appear to be in print (in the paperback edition), so could be found via "brick & mortar" channels, but the Amazon new/used vendors currently have "new" copies available for as little as $5.75 (on an $18.95 cover price book), so if you were wanting to add it to your library, I'd say go with that

Notes:
1. http://btripp-books.livejournal.com/34691.html
2. http://btripp-books.livejournal.com/5520.html
3-4. http://amzn.to/29SVH6r

Thursday, May 24, 2007[1]

another "attraction" approach ...

I had Dr. Wayne W. Dyer's The Power of Intention: Learning to Co-create Your World Your Way[2] recommended to me as being less "newagey" than many of the "laws of attraction" books that I've been beating myself over the head with of late, and I will admit that, for the most part, it's not as fluffy as the others. However, I never quite was able to get into synch with this. Dyer goes for substantial chunks of this sounding very reasonable, providing applicable "coaching" for various approaches to intention, but then will drop in something that seemed (to me, at least) to come completely out of left field.

Now, over the years when I was publishing "metaphysical" books, I had to wade through a whole lot of B.S. to get to the things that I felt were of sufficient value to actually get into print, so maybe I'm a bit *sensitive* about stuff that is pretending to be "science" but isn't. I was rather disappointed to find Dyer using "resistance testing" as a basis of saying that "studies have *proven*" some thing or another ... I've seen enough of this to have no confidence that it *proves* anything. I also had the "B.S. meter" redlining when he quoted "research" as to how "high-energy people counterbalance the negative effect of low-energy people", complete with "levels of vibration" and impressive-looking numbers (with no evident substance) for how many "negative" people would be balanced for each "higher" person. It's a shame that a book that *didn't need* this sort of crap is tainted with it.

On the positive side, The Power of Intention[3] has some fairly practical advice for "aligning with the source" (much like concepts of the Tao), and being able to bring that "creative energy" into one's life. Unfortunately, the *useful* parts are burdened with all the "newage" baggage. One part that I particularly didn't "get" was the "Seven Faces of Intention", a concept that Dyer outlines over a few pages in an early chapter, and then refers to offhandedly at random times through the rest of the book, as if this was something *functional* like gravity or magnetism! These "seven faces" are creativity, kindness, love, beauty, expansion, abundance, and receptivity ... but what than "means" as a symbolic unit never becomes particularly clear.

Now, this sounds like I didn't like the book, which is not exactly true. I found his approach to energy, perception, awareness, the whole "source" concept, etc. very interesting, and fairly useful (in fact, putting Tolle's The Power of Now[4] into the context of this book made those concepts far less muddled) ... it's just that it would have been so much *better* had the egregious twaddle (as discussed above) been edited out! I will admit that there were times where Dyer was drifting into that "no abundance for *you*" believe-or-be-screwed stuff (ala The Secret[5]) but on the whole his focus on constantly steering away from "low energy" thoughts and behavior patterns made this a whole lot less strident and far easier to put into practice!.

I see that this was presented in some form on public TV, and I wonder how *that* played out ... needless to say, it's still in print, so should be available at your local bookstore if you want to get a "retail" copy. The good news of the media exposure it had is that there are tons of copies out in the new/used channel, with "like new" copies available (at the time I'm writing this) for under a buck via some of the Amazon vendors (and "new" copies for only $2). I might be hesitant to recommend this at the $25 cover price, but being that it can be obtained for so little cash at the moment, I'd say "go for it" ... it certainly is one of the *better* "law of attraction" books that I've seen, so it could be a good place to start if you were wanting to look into that genre.

Notes:

1. http://btripp-books.livejournal.com/35018.html
2-3. http://amzn.to/29Rbh35
4. http://btripp-books.livejournal.com/34364.html
5. http://btripp-books.livejournal.com/33791.html

Thursday, May 24, 2007[1]

Blew through this one ...

Yes, for those of you paying *way* too close attention to the goings-on of this space, this is, indeed, the *second* book review penned today. Since it only took me a couple of days to plow through this volume (as opposed to two weeks for the Dyer book reviewed earlier today), and I didn't want my recall of it to "get cold" over the course of the holiday weekend, I figured I'd just get this done now.

Frankly, I don't really know *why* I ended up reading Rhonda Britten's Fearless Living: Live without Excuses and Love without Regret[2] ... the "how", I have a handle on, though. You see, I had been trying to get some time to "pick the brain" of an old acquaintance of mine regarding details of setting up a counseling practice, and he recommended his cousin Rhonda's book, saying that a lot of what I needed to know could be found in there. So, I dutifully ordered a copy of it, and set it in the stack to be read. Unfortunately, there was even *less* information on the ins and outs of running such a venture in *this* than there had been in that insufferable Shelly Stockwell book that I wrote about[3] last month!

In a phrase that regular readers are no doubt sick of hearing, "this is not to say this is a *bad* book", but it was not what I had been expecting to get into, and so was both a bit of an irritation and disappointment.

Personally, I would have *preferred* to not have followed up the Dyer book with this, in terms of "where things are going" in my head. Whereas Dyer spends a lot of time coaching the reader to disengage from "low energy" thought forms, Britten has a tendency to almost *wallow* in a quicksand of emotions and fixations on past events in her life. Fearless Living[4] reminds me of a "chick flick" ... while it may be well done, and have solid points, its tone is just too *Fried Green Tomatoes* for my tastes. Now, Britten's "system" (also called "Fearless Living") that she outlines in the book does seem to be very well structured, with useful exercises, helpful guidance, etc., (and interesting paradigms of "the wheel of fear" and the "wheel of freedom"), but it all seems to be targeted to people who are having major emotional "issues".

Britten, herself, has had to deal with *serious* emotional trauma, and she spends *a lot* of the book dragging the reader through these various scenarios. While I'm sure this was quite therapeutic for the author, I'm not sure *why* all this extensive "sharing" is in there unless she's trying to "build empathy" with her readers. As I did not come to this book looking to salve some psychic wound, though, it does seem like a whole lot of unproductive verbiage which immerses her audience in a lot of negative emotion ... and, for what? ... showing her readers that she's had it bad too? ... that she understands? ... what? The effect is that of a "self-help" book crossed with a pathos-soaked autobiography, and just reeks of "TMI".

Much as I wish that one could retroactively edit the Dyer book to remove the "newage twaddle" bits, I feel that this would be a *much* stronger book if Britten would have left her own scarring experiences at the door. It's fine to take a "clinical" look at your clients' stories, but to constantly be dipping back into your own history for stuff (that in some cases make you seem *clueless*!) you've been through begs the question: *is this a book to help others, or to make "poor Rhonda" feel better about herself?*

Again, the actual *system* that Britten details in the book looks fairly decent, but it's too bad that it takes so much "filtering" to sift the substantial bits from the tear-jerker autobiography. Of course, I'm sure there is a *significant* demographic who would find this viscous mix quite appealing, but I am (thankfully) not among them. As noted, there *is* useful material in this book, and if you're interested in checking it out, it does still appear to be in print in the paperback edition, with used copies of the hardback running around three bucks via the usual suspects. Just to let you know, this has a five-star rating over on Amazon, so there are a lot of folks who think it's just *marvy* ... so you might want to take that into consideration as a counter-point to my typical bitter cynicism!

Notes:

http://btripp-books.livejournal.com/35251.html

http://amzn.to/29Raqzl

http://btripp-books.livejournal.com/32954.html

http://amzn.to/29Raqzl

Friday, June 1, 2007[1]

Almost didn't add this one ...

As I've noted previously[2], there are not a lot of "business" books in my library, and things like this rarely get counted as even "reading", being more a research project than anything else, so don't make it onto my bookshelves, nor into LibraryThing[3], or even mentioned in here. However, unexpectedly, Blythe Camenson's Careers for New Agers & Other Cosmic Types[4] did a better job of giving me those "pointers" for setting up a metaphysical consulting practice than any of the books that I had specifically bought for such info, so I figured I'd give it a Place In My Library. Ms. Camenson seems to have carved out a niche of writing vast lots of "Careers for" and "Great Jobs for" and "Opportunities in" books, with a fill-in-the-blank for personality types, college majors, and various professional fields, with 75 titles listed on Amazon. So, it's not too surprising that this volume is a bit on the "skimming" side, and is rather an "outsider's view" (I think her "expert" books are the ones she has about getting things published!).

The book is broken up into sections roughly along the lines of "mind", "body", "teaching", etc., with a few "career paths" noted in each. Some of her choices seem odd, but this is several years old (think of how much has changed on the Internet in the past 7 years), and she seems to not have an "insider's grasp" on the "new age" world, resulting in some very minor areas getting more attention than they might otherwise have, and some rather major areas being glossed over. I was rather amused that she dedicated a whole chapter to being a Paranormal Investigator, which seems to have blossomed as a TV staple in recent years, but at the time of writing was somewhat limited (oooh, *she must by psychic!*).

Again, while I did find some of the information in here useful, it's certainly a book for a limited audience. I found it interesting that she considered *event planning* a "new age career" and had it bundled in with teaching and consulting. Go figure. Anyway, the paperback appears to still be in print, so could be found via your favorite brick & mortar bookstore (oddly, Amazon has this at full cover with no discount), but "like new" copies can be had via the new/used vendors for as little as 75¢ plus shipping (in fact, I only ordered this because it *was* so cheap when I was poking around online for some other career books!). If you're looking for info on the subject, you could certainly do worse.

Notes:

1. http://btripp-books.livejournal.com/35426.html

2. http://btripp-books.livejournal.com/21716.html

3. http://btripp-books.com/

4. http://amzn.to/29Ltr3X

Monday, June 11, 2007[1]

Well, here's the last of these ...

Yes, long-time readers of this space have no doubt been asking *"What the heck has gotten into Brendan?"* for the run of "newagey" books that I've been beating myself over the head with during the past couple of months. As previously noted, this has been a conscious attempt to both try to change my outlook (especially on the job search, which had been constantly threatening to turn into a downward spiral of anguish, frustration, and despair), and to give that whole "The Secret" thing of playing the attraction/intent game with the Universe a decent shot. If you want to see a run-down of these titles, just go over to my LibraryThing catalog[2].

Anyway, the current book, Esther & Jerry Hicks' The Law of Attraction: The Basics of the Teachings of Abraham[3], was a late addition to the list, largely due to one reader's insistence on how well the Hicks' teachings have helped her. Now, I'm not sure that this is the *specific* book she intended, but it seemed a logical starting point (being "The Basics") and it does present itself as an over-view of their "system".

As I have also frequently pointed out, I am not a great fan of "channeled" books, and this one really demands a certain degree of credulity for that sort of thing, as Esther Hicks suddenly (well, after reading the similarly generated "Seth" books) began to communicate for "Abraham" (no, not the Biblical patriarch, but some "group entity" from a disembodied plane of being) with husband Jerry playing the Larry King role with pre-scripted "interview questions". Interestingly, I've heard that the Hicks were in the initial editions of The Secret[4], but got edited out to make the book more "Oprah-friendly" (I guess "life coaches" play better to the daytime TV audience than "disincarnate entities").

While The Law of Attraction[5] is better *structured* than most of these books (its "system" is in four parts: The *Law of Attraction™*, The *Science of Deliberate Creation™*, The *Art of Allowing™*, and *Segment Intending™*) it still depends *heavily* on a rather simplistic emotional spectrum, i.e., if you're "Happy" you're doing the right thing and will attract what you desire, but if you're *not* "Happy", you're messing up and are only going to be drawing in more stuff you don't want (this is their *Emotional Guidance System*, which somehow managed to not be trademarked). They even address this, in a section that reminded me of Robin William's Peter Pan in the movie Hook[6], where it recommends finding the "one happy thought" (or activity) to get you in a happy place (not necessarily to *fly*, of course).

Another book which frequently came to mind while reading this one was, remarkably, Ayn Rand's The Virtue of Selfishness[7], as what "Abraham" counsels is very much a *"I create the Universe I live in."* view, and the only person that you can do anything for or about is yourself. In fact, "Abraham" insists (the book uses plural verbs for the "group being", but it just looked stupid in this context) that there are no such thing as "victims" and that on some level the individual has *attracted* whatever bad stuff that has happened to them ... from traffic accidents to muggings, from critical illness to stock market crashes. Frankly, the whole "Abraham" system could be described as a new age philosophy of Solipsism[8] (leaving aside the general solipsistic tendency of *everything* "newage"), although with just enough Objectivism to not deny the physical world *exists*!

Again, the Hicks' system is sufficiently well-structured that it is at least *plausible* as a template for personal action, which puts it a leg up on most of its fellow "attraction" plans. The book is in the format of an on-going "interview", with questions being framed by Jerry and being answered (in various lengths) by "Abraham" via Esther, and has every topic listed in the table of contents, making it easy to refer back to. The most "unique" part of the system, I found, was the admonition to not even *think* of negative things or outcomes, which puts it into that Scarlett O'Hara zone (*"I can't think about that right now."*) but begs the question of *how* exactly one can banish the normal "risk assessment" cognitions, let alone the extreme memetic intrusions (try not to think of a pink elephant). The *Segment Intending*™ part seems to be designed to address this (breaking one's timeline into segments which each have their own mental frame, from brushing one's teeth to driving to work, etc.), but it sounds remarkably complicated.

I usually can say that I got some particular useful tidbit from one of these books, but I'm not sure I can point to anything in particular that I'm taking away from The Law of Attraction[9] except for a vague sense of *"gee, maybe it's OK to be selfish/solipsistic!"* ... as always, Your Mileage May Vary.

In a rare and brash fit of "intention", I actually paid *cover price* (plus tax) for this at a newagey brick-and-mortar store. You, however, might do better via Amazon, who have it at a 32% discount ... not much help from the new/used vendors, though, as their prices (plus shipping) are over Amazon's, so better to combine a couple of books and get the free shipping if this sounded like something that you might find useful.

Notes:

1. http://btripp-books.livejournal.com/35829.html
2. http://btripp-books.com/
3. http://amzn.to/2ajcVYy
4. http://btripp-books.livejournal.com/33791.html
5. http://amzn.to/2ajcVYy
6. http://imdb.com/title/tt0102057/
7. http://amzn.to/29MrzZT
8. http://en.wikipedia.org/wiki/Solipsism
9. http://amzn.to/2ajcVYy

Tuesday, June 12, 2007[1]

That's more like it ...

As noted repeatedly, I had been, over the past month or so, sort of "beating myself over the head" with various new age tomes intended to improve my attitude about stuff and perhaps set me on the road towards "attracting" prosperity. While those about me have noticed a certain attitude adjustment, we are still waiting on the Big Cash Payoff part of this. While we are, to borrow a joke from the Dalai Lama, "Waiting for Lotto" (or that fabulous new job that will pay well and not be a soul-crushing grind), I'm going back to reading books that don't make me roll my eyes and mimic retching sounds.

Fortunately, Christopher Hitchens' Letters to a Young Contrarian[2] is a breath of bracing fresh air compared to the patchouli sludge I've been figuratively exposed to of late. Somewhat patterned on Rilke's *Letters to a Young Poet*, this is Hitchens' meeting the challenge made to him of creating some sort of a mentoring guide (indeed, this is part of the "Art of Mentoring" series of books) for being something of a gadfly, activist, etc. In a score of "letters", Hitchens skips around from topic to topic, but never veering too far from his central tenet of developing and studiously protecting a certain level of intellectual honesty.

Hitchens is a bit of an odd fellow, in that he does seem to practice what he preaches along these lines. While author of a good many titles, at least half of them are, like this one (coming in at 141 pages), more in the tradition of philosophical or political pamphlets or tracts than "books" per se. Until just recently he had only shown up on *my* radar with his similarly brief savaging of the Clintons, *No One Left To Lie To* ... needless to say, I found that a stalwart of the Left taking apart Bubba and Hitlery was quite a sight to behold, and he certainly got points from me for that effort. Of course, many will find it odd that I can be as much of a fan of Hitchens as I am of Ann Coulter, but both of them bring to the table a level of clarity that I respect (and a poison prose that I admire), while carrying baggage (his Leftism, her Xtianity) that I'm willing to ignore.

As Letters to a Young Contrarian[3] is "all over the map" subject-wise, I thought I'd share some quotes that I found particularly arch to provide a sense of the general thrust of Hitchens' writing:

> Discussing the atmosphere of the mid-1950's:
>
> "... a time when existential anomie was trading at an inflated price."
>
> From a section on how "public opinion" is variously manipulated for the benefit of those in power:
>
> "... the forces of piety have always and everywhere been the sworn enemy of the open mind and the open book."

And, in his closing admonitions:

> *"Seek out argument and disputation for their own sake; the grave will provide plenty of time for silence."*

The whole book is beautifully written, with well-crafted words wrapping up cutting barbs aimed at assorted hypocrisies. Of course, Mr. Hitchens is currently the "boogie man *du jour*" for the rabid Xtian crowd, and he does not disappoint in his animosity towards blind belief. In fact, I think that this may be the only place I've actually encountered the term "antitheist" outside of the antitheism[4] community on LiveJournal (which is also where I initially found this book recommended), a term he uses (differentiating from agnosticism or atheism) to define his stance that all faiths are essentially built on lies and that religion is in and of itself harmful.

He references many authors that I have not yet read, and I've been able to put together quite a weighty "wish list" while reading this. As a particular *lagniappe*, he also introduced me (sitting in for his purported correspondent) to the rather delightful *Microcosmographia Academica*[5], a satiric 1908 guide to the internal politics of the University, which seems to be as pointed today as it was a century ago!

Needless to say, I *highly* recommend Letters to a Young Contrarian[6]. It is currently in print, so should be available via your local brick-and-mortar vendor, but is also on Amazon for a couple of bucks off of cover price. You could save a bit going with the new/used vendors, but due to the low retail (befitting a book under 150 pages!), you probably won't be getting a "steal" (especially when shipping on those deals is already 31% of the full price). Anyway ... no matter the distribution channel you chose, *get this book!* It really is that good.

Notes:

1. http://btripp-books.livejournal.com/35925.html
2-3. http://amzn.to/2ajcKNa
4. http://antitheism.livejournal.com/
5. http://en.wikipedia.org/wiki/Microcosmographia_Academica
6. http://amzn.to/2ajcKNa

Tuesday, June 19, 2007[1]

How odd ...

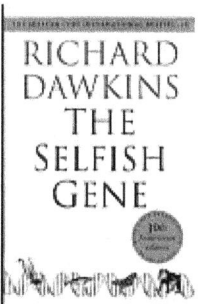

This may be the most "popular" book that I've read over the past several years ... there are 1,780 folks on Library-Thing[2] who have a copy, and 22 of them have already penned reviews. While I enjoyed reading this well enough, I really didn't get much "new" from it (which, I suppose, it not remarkable as this is the "30th Anniversary Edition", meaning that the concepts in it have been kicking around for quite a while), just more details to things "I already knew" for the most part.

I've been trying to "find an angle" for a review here, and am, frankly, coming up a bit dry. I would certainly *recommend* Richard Dawkins' The Selfish Gene[3] to all and sundry as a very good basic book on the concept of genetics and what that whole group of ideas means, although many will no doubt find the basic thread (that people, like all "living beings", are simply machines developed by genes to ensure their survival and propagation) somewhat less than engaging. Now, I'm hardly the "religious" type, but I must admit coming away from this book feeling a bit, well ... irrelevant. Not only do the individual carriers of the genes not really matter except as a vehicle *for* those genes, but the idea that after not very many generations the recognizable inheritance of the individual is so diluted that it becomes almost meaningless. Frankly, I wish to have *meaning*, and I guess that's the rub on Dawkin's approach ... the individual plant, animal, etc., doesn't ultimately seem to have *any*.

On a brighter note, The Selfish Gene[4] is chock full of *fascinating* tidbits (such as all the aphids on a particular plant are likely to be the "clone" offspring of a single mother, and are genetically identical, and could be thought of as a single *entity* expressed over a hundred or so discreet packages), and is a very interesting read. While intentionally shying away from going into the mathematics behind the science, there are some quite detailed looks at "game theory" elements like the classic "Prisoner's Dilemma" which are here used to chart out "evolutionary stable strategies" dealing with such things as in-group altruism and inter-species cooperation. Also, some of those inter-species arrangements (especially in the insect kingdom) that are described here *are* quite remarkable. I was also amazed to find that the very familiar Internet term "meme" was originated by Dawkins 30-some years ago to describe a self-replicating concept (the example he tracks was an attribution error in the title of a work that spread from two initial mis-typings to be a common error in the literature ... it would be interesting to see what he thinks of the like of "L.J. memes" so prevalent in "social networking" sites today).

The "30th Anniversary Edition" has two extra chapters which bring some of the ideas up to current understanding, and there are rather extensive notes (one chapter had almost as many pages of notes as there were of text), putting some of what had originally been written into a broader context of academic development on the subjects being addressed. I make this distinction in part due to the fact that used copies of the *old* edition are going at a fraction of what the new one is. In fact, at this writing, there is only about a buck separating the lowest used price from Amazon's discounted price ... and you'd be paying shipping on top of that for the used copy. While this is no doubt sitting on the shelves of your favorite brick-and-mortar book vendor, your best bet might well be Amazon (which has it new at 37% off of cover) if combined with other stuff to get free shipping.

Notes:

1. http://btripp-books.livejournal.com/36158.html
2. http://btripp-books.com/
3-4. http://amzn.to/29DdXBO

Sunday, June 24, 2007[1]

A good one ...

I was mentally writing a *rave* review of this book when I was about half way done with it, and, in fact, 2/3rds of it is fantastic ... unfortunately, the last section was a serious let-down, so I'm left with a quandary as to how to approach this review.

As noted, the first two parts of Timothy Ferris' The Mind's Sky: Human Intelligence in a Cosmic Context[2] are very good. In the first he looks at the cosmos, our relationship to it, the drive for communication, how galactic-level cultures might appear and survive, etc., and in the second he looks at the human mind, how the brain functions, and how we are a complex of various types of "intelligences". This latter is very interesting, quoting studies that show that the "conscious mind" acts as something of a "press agent" for the whole, attempting to put a unified and intentional front on actions which are not necessarily volitionally made. Also looking at how different types of intelligence often "compete for space" in the limited real estate of the brain, with several fascinating examples. I really wish he had simply taken these two parts and done a "wrap it all up" last section to the book.

Unfortunately, the third part of the book sounds almost petulant, and has elements that have not "aged well" over the 15 years since this was written. As regular readers of these reviews will recall, I've recently been catching up on my reading from books bought in the early 1990's and there has been a lot of times when I've found the stuff I'm looking at *hopelessly* dated, especially from a computer basis. That's one aspect here, as is his addressing "political" hot-button issues from 1991 which seem almost quaint at this remove. I don't suppose that one can really *fault* an author for writing "in time", but it was a rather stark contrast of how good the first two parts of this book are compared to the final section.

Again, the main thrust of this book is *fascinating*, the concept of intelligence and where it might stand in relation to the universe at large. One very interesting point Ferris makes is that "intelligence", in the way we generally think of it, might not be such an "inevitable" development of life. From a standpoint of something like SETI, this would be defined as the ability to send and receive radio signals, and there were many millions of years of quite extensive *life* on this planet without that happening, and even over the course of the presence of "modern humans", this ability has only manifested over the past century. The Mind's Sky[3] suggests that "intelligence" is a particular adaptation to planetary environmental stressors, and only made possible on Earth by the impact events which eradicated the dinosaurs and allowed for the spread of various mammals (including those that developed opposable thumbs and fine-control digits for transport through trees), and the Ice Ages which appear to have favored Homo Sapiens over its various "cousins". The question is left on the table about just how frequently *does* "intelligence" arise ... only on planets with enough chaos to elicit its development, but not so much to eradicate it before it can flourish?

Anyway, this is a worthwhile book to pick up, despite the let-down of the third section. It appears that a "reprint" edition of this is still out there, so might be available at your local brick-and-mortar book vendor, but you can get a "very good" copy of the original hardcover from the Amazon new/used guys for a measly $0.01 (plus $3.99 shipping), which is what I'd suggest were you interested in adding this to your collection!

Notes:

1. http://btripp-books.livejournal.com/36490.html

2-3. http://amzn.to/2ajbl92

Wednesday, June 27, 2007[1]

Oh, and this ...

I may have mentioned being a bit on the obsessive-compulsive side, and every once and a while this will manifest in my reading choices. I just recently transferred the books from the boxes under my desk (where "recently read" stuff goes before it gets "filed" on a shelf, which is why there's typically a significant lag between when books in my LibraryThing catalog[2] get their "finished" tag and their "filed" tag) onto a cleared-out shelf, and found that I had space for a smallish book. All the stuff that I am currently reading would be too big to fit, so I was in a bit of a quandary. However, in the process of digging out the front bathroom (a long story), I uncovered a number of books "abandoned" a couple of years back when that got turned into "storage", and among those was David Bergland's Libertarianism In One Lesson[3], which was just about the right thickness needed for the shelf. So, to the top of the reading priority list it went, and I pretty much blew through it in 3 sessions over the course of the weekend.

Now, I realize that this is sounds like "I wouldn't have read this otherwise", but that's not really the case. I'd picked this up back when I was very active in the local Libertarian Party, and it was just something "to get around to". Frankly, I have recently been trying to *avoid* "political" books, as they've been tending to get me upset ... and this is no exception to that rule. If one is of a Libertarian "personal freedom" bent, one can not help to feel how *doomed* we are as a people given the way our government has been wiping its ass with the Constitution over the past fifty years or so (heck, it could be argued that said ass-wiping started with Lincoln, but that's another story), and any book that systematically puts forth what SHOULD be happening is likely to highlight the vast discrepancies between where we're heading and where we really ought to want to go!

Bergland has been involved in the Libertarian Party pretty much from its start, and was the V.P. candidate on the 1976 ticket. This book is something of an "evolving document", the copy that I have is the 8th edition (from 2000), and it's now available in a much-revised 9th edition[4], and the focus of the book seems to be frequently updated (since its early-80's origin) to reflect the current trends and issues ... which is a *good thing* for a book like this, obviously.

Organized somewhat like a collection of "position papers", the books gives some basic background on Libertarianism, its philosophical foundations, etc., and then starts dealing with particular subjects, from health care to prohibition, from 2nd Amendment rights to education, and so forth. There is one key phrase that Bergland uses throughout which is *"Utopia is NOT an option."* ... as it seems that the most frequent arguments that come up against Libertarian ideas are based on totally unattainable Utopian ideals. Either you have personal freedom or you don't, in the real world the "don't" side of the equation leads down a road of ever-increasingly coercive government and not to some perfect State. The other key concept is the old adage that "there is no free lunch", as everything needs to be paid for at some level, and either *you* pay for what you need/use/want or you are ultimately having the government steal it (via the threat of armed violence, aka the IRS) from somebody else. You can pretty much peg the Libertarian stance on any issue by triangulating from these two catch-phrases.

Personally, I do not agree with everything in this book. I think that Bergland's stance about borders (totally open) is suicidal as a society (I tend towards the "Heinlein Libertarian" camp which is strongly Libertarian for those who qualify ... citizens who have proven their responsibility ... but defensive to those outside of the culture). Unfortunately, this is pretty much the problem that the L.P. has in general ... while folks might agree with 75% of the Libertarian ideal, the remaining 25% becomes fodder for mocking and out-of-context attacks. This is why the phrases *"There is no free lunch."* and *"Utopia is not an option."* become so useful, as they focus in on the *reasons* that one might support stuff that on the surface looks a bit "iffy". I did, however, want to send copies of this off to my *elected representatives* (like it would do any good with *that* bunch of leftist yahoos) as soon as I finished reading it!

Anyway, the book is currently in print, but not in the stores (as far as I can tell), and Amazon has copies via secondary vendors going for as little as a buck (the new 9th edition[5] is at full cover at $11.95). If you have *any* interest in personal freedom and limiting the choking hold that the government has on us, I'd highly recommend picking up a copy.

Notes:

1. http://btripp-books.livejournal.com/36630.html
2. http://btripp-books.com/
3-5. http://amzn.to/29LjfMQ

Saturday, July 7, 2007[1]

Long time ...

Some books just take me a long time to plow through ... this being one of them, having been started in early April, and not finished until the end of June. Of course, in that same period I read 15 other books, so it was more a factor of this "niche" (it was back in my "office reading chair" area) being neglected than any particular density of difficulty.

In fact, Leonard Shlain's Art & Physics: Parallel Visions in Space, Time, and Light[2] is quite interesting and engaging. Contrary to what one might expect, Shlain is *neither* an Artist nor a Physicist, but a Surgeon, and the book arose from his efforts to *explain* modern art to his pre-teen daughter, who was not "getting" it in a series of museum visits. As he delved into some art history to be able to communicate these concepts to his kid, he began to realize that what he was reading about art over the past hundred or so years reminded him of his other readings of the advent of modern theories in physics.

Of course, to really understand *modern* art, one has to go all the way back to the roots of *Western* art, and so Art & Physics[3] begins with Greek philosophers and moves on from there. Each chapter is titled in a "This / That" format, sometimes being as blatant as taking a specific art movement and putting it in the context of an area of physics (such as "Cubism / Space") and sometimes being more general discursive categories (i.e. "Sacred / Profane"). Although his focus *is* in the visual arts, examples are also woven through from literature and psychology.

Make no mistake, his thesis is *fascinating*, and the argument he puts forth for something of a *zeitgeist*, (especially in how parallel developments in art and science *do* appear to have been generated without any "cross-pollination" between the artists and scientists) is quite compelling, but he throws a bit of a curve in at the end, which makes the book as a whole a bit less than satisfying. Had Shlain simply "tied up the loose ends" and written a unifying closing chapter, this would have perhaps been "a better *book*", however instead of going that route, he opts to follow the ellipses into a more "mystical" territory, trying to sort out art and physics in terms of the brain, and awareness (seemingly evolving along dual tracks in the culture) in terms of the mind, and then (as though to close the circle back to the start of the book) in "Dionysus / Apollo" taking a *psychological* look at the early Greek Gods as models of developing mental states, and coming out with: *"By extrapolation, I propose that spacetime generates **universal mind**."*

I am, certainly, not opposed to theorizing along these lines, only it leave the reader hanging in a "Twilight Zone" scenario, where one had been on a train nearly into the station and suddenly having veered off past the signpost into a whole 'nuther reality. I really wish that Shlain had "finished" Art & Physics[4] as noted above, and *then* come up with a follow-up book where he takes these ideas and supports them in the sort of depth that he uses for the "art and physics" part of this. While fascinating, this sort of "just happens" at the end, and leaves everything open-ended and adrift.

Anyway, aside from this caveat, I found the book quite good, and it's something that is well worth picking up if you have an interest in either part of its title. It does appear to still be in print, so could be found at your local book vendor, but there are copies available via the Amazon new/used guys in "like new" condition for under three bucks.

Notes:

1. http://btripp-books.livejournal.com/37023.html
2-4. http://amzn.to/29QLszs

Sunday, July 8, 2007[1]

another ...

Here's another of those books that re-surfaced when we dug out the front bathroom ... I recall having this sitting around a while, but I don't recall *buying* it, which makes me think (along with the retail stickers on it) that it came from my late Mother several years back.

As I've noted previously, I don't really read "business books", and this is on the border of being one of those. As opposed to those "newagey" positive-think books I read a month or so back, this is coming out from the "INJOY Group", which appears to be one of those suppliers of rah-rah business meeting speakers, including it's author, John C. Maxwell. The 21 Indispensable Qualities of a Leader: Becoming the Person Others Will Want to Follow[2] is at least brief and to the point (albeit seemingly a follow-up to another "21" book Maxwell had previously released on "Leadership"), being, not surprisingly, structured in 21 chapters, each with a couple of more-or-less to-theme quotes, a "story" about a leader who manifested that particular quality, a "Fleshing It Out" section with key points of that quality broken out, a "Reflecting On It" section with questions to ask yourself about how you exhibit (or not) that quality, a "Bringing It Home" section with something of a to-do list to work on that quality, and a "Daily Take-Away" section which generally deals with some public figure who did something which illustrates the quality being discussed in that chapter. Maxwell suggests spreading the 21 chapters out over a month or so to be able to "work" through each (yeah, I just read through it).

So, what are these "indispensable qualities" a leader should have? Here's the list: Character, Charisma, Commitment, Communication, Competence, Courage, Discernment, Focus, Generosity, Initiative, Listening, Passion, Positive Attitude, Problem Solving, Relationships, Responsibility, Security, Self-Discipline, Servanthood, Teachability, and Vision. Unfortunately, much like those "positive attitude" books (oh, look, it's there *again*), if you're deficient in any of these areas, you fail as a leader. Although the book *is* structured to allow one to work on oneself, the *attitude* seems far more dismissive for those who don't already "measure up".

So, would I recommend The 21 Indispensable Qualities of a Leader[3]? I guess so ... again, it's "not my kind of thing", but I admire its *structure*, and found some of the bits and pieces in it quite fascinating (I've especially glommed onto one of the quotes, from anthropologist Margaret Mead: *"What people say, what people do, and what they say they do are entirely different things."*) ... of course, if the self-help genre is your cup of tea, this will likely be one of your favorite books (it certainly has a bunch of 5-star raves on its Amazon page). Speaking of Amazon, this is still in print (so might well be at your local brick & mortar bookstore) and they have this for about 1/3rd off of cover, which is likely as good as you're likely to do on it, as it's about a wash (with shipping) on what their new/used vendors are currently offering.

Notes:
1. http://btripp-books.livejournal.com/37362.html
2-3. http://amzn.to/29KNHqd

Monday, July 9, 2007[1]

Settle down!

Oh, come *on* already ... when I started *writing* this, I could HEAR the undies of my more liberal readers already tightening up into knots! Yes, it's a book by *the boogieman*, get over it.

Sheesh.

Actually, it's too bad that more folks *won't* read this book, as it is quite good, and the points being raised are important. To be honest, I probably wouldn't have read this myself (I'm not very likely to go buy a book by a "TV person"), but this was another of those that was passed along to me by my Mom, and it was sitting out in the front bathroom, and it got picked up out of sheer convenience. I'm not a huge fan of Bill O'Reilly, as I do *try* to keep myself on an even emotional keel, and watching "confrontational" TV (especially dealing with subjects on which I have a strong opinion) just gets me pointlessly worked up, but this book is a context where his *clarity* is not bogged down by his combativeness. However, in Who's Looking Out for You?[2] O'Reilly pretty much deals with the stuff that gets *him* worked up (so there are bits that are somewhat "ranty"), based on a unifying theme of finding out who you can or can not trust to have your best interests at heart.

I was not expecting this book to be as autobiographical as it is. O'Reilly takes the theme and walks through a lot of his own life showing times when he was "stupid" about what he did or who he trusted. Along the way he tackles Race, Religion, the Media, Education, Government, and *Lawyers* (a quote:*"The American justice system is a runaway money train where those without legal credentials are tied to the tracks."*), among others, clearing the smokescreens that cover up ugly truths.

Now, as regular readers know, I'm a Libertarian, especially in the sense of being very conservative on most issues of governance, but rather liberal on individual rights issues. Part of my personal "spin" is that I'm somewhat "anti-theistic", holding that Religion in general is a Bad Thing. O'Reilly (like Ms. Coulter) comes from a diametrically opposite stance, holding that Religion is very important, and especially *that* one. As such, I find some of the places that O'Reilly goes in Who's Looking Out for You?[3] are needlessly "preachy", although he is at least *tolerant* towards opinions on the subject dissenting from his.

Unfortunately, I doubt many folks of the liberal/left bent would even attempt to read this (and would likely bust blood vessels in the process were they to make the effort), and for the conservatives, it's pretty much what they already know. From where I sit, most of this book is no *surprise*, just a clear exposition of a lot of "what's wrong in the world". Frankly, the only "revelation" was that O'Reilly stands 6'4" tall (hard to gauge that when you've only seen him behind a desk on TV!) ... which leads to a lot of amusing thoughts of "Death Match" scenarios with various irritants from the Left!

Anyway, I enjoyed reading Who's Looking Out for You?[4] and would certainly recommend it, with the caveats detailed above. Lucky for you, this is one of those which can be had for a *steal*. While it is still in print (so could be found in your local bookstore) and Amazon has it at 27% off cover price, the new/used vendors have *lots* of "very good" copies for *a penny* (plus the $3.99 shipping, of course) and there are "like new" copies for as low as fifty cents. Such a deal!

Notes:

1. http://btripp-books.livejournal.com/37579.html

2-4. http://amzn.to/29KZcdg

Monday, July 9, 2007[1]

Hoooo-boy ...

I don't know where to *start* on this one ... I guess the mundane stuff. This was another of my "coffee table books" from my pre-marriage apartment that got stuffed in a box when we moved and only re-surfaced when we dug out the front bathroom (which had devolved into storage space ... long story), so it's been "hanging around" for quite a while now. Mayan Vision Quest: Mystical Initiation in Mesoamerica[2] is primarily a book of photos, but is SO over-the-edge "newagey" that it boggles the mind. Frankly, I was *planning* on writing a much more derisive review, but did a bit of digging on the authors, and began to get at least a glimmer of where this was "coming from".

My first gripe here is that the photos are 90% shot on infrared film. Now, this came out in 1991, a long time before TV discovered that you could shoot in "night vision" and make everything all spooky and thereby spew out dozens of unbelievably lame "ghost hunter" shows which are nearly totally dependent on the effects that produces ... so I can hardly blame Cynthia MacAdams for using a cliché, although her *intent* is exactly the same as the TV producers'! The photos are all in greyscale, with varying degrees of excessive granularity (there are maybe 3 pictures in the whole book which are "sharp"), and all those tell-tale signs of IR film, dark-to-black skies, bright white foliage, etc., all done to *"capture the mystical forces in the pyramids and temples"*. Ohhh-kayy.

MacAdams was the photographer for Mayan Vision Quest[2], with the words perpetrated by Hunbartz Men and Charles Bensinger (both, interestingly, mis-spelled in the Amazon listings). The text is a "real doozy" ... frankly, back in my publishing days I wouldn't have touched this because it's so "out there". I started to poke around and found that Bensinger is a "newage" writer, specializing in Green politics and revisionist histories, and Men is *"a Mayan Elder and Daykeeper"* who supposedly is the holder of *"the sacred teachings that were hidden by the Mayan priesthood shortly after the Spanish Conquistadors landed in Mexico in 1519"* despite the Classic Mayan culture being dead half a millennia at that point, and even the post-Classic Mayan/Toltec culture having collapsed a couple of hundred years before! At least that explains where they were getting specifics of who was doing what in which buildings ... ala *"In the upper section of this pyramid seven priests would conduct rituals to the seven solar systems."* (???) or *"To enhance the rituals performed here, colors were changed to ensure the optimum energy flow through the structure."* ... for structures that had laid in ruins for a thousand years.

Now, I'm not one to openly mock another's Shamanism or "ancient knowledge", but the chronology of Hunbartz Men's "sacred teachings" should tax the "suspension of disbelief" of all but the most credulous new ager. Frankly, I suspect that Ms. MacAdams falls into *that* category, and Mr. Bensinger is the type of writer who's never met a lie he didn't like, as long as it made Western Civilization look bad. Again, I (having read quite a lot of historical/archaeological material about the Maya) was *aghast* at the text accompanying the "ooh, *spooky*" pictures in this book!

Needless to say, I find this hard to recommend, except, perhaps, as a stellar example of over-blown newage twaddle. As much as I love "armchair traveling" through a book of ruin photos, this is even a tainted experience on that level, as all the photos are (by way of their grainy IR effects) *bad*, if well-composed and of interesting subjects. I am relieved to see that this is, indeed, out of print, so you would have to go looking through the aftermarket if for some reason you were interested in picking up a copy. There *are* some to be had via the Amazon new/used vendors (for as little as 70¢ for a "good" copy and six bucks and change for a "like new" one), if you think this needs to be in your library ... but you *have* been warned!

Notes:

1. http://btripp-books.livejournal.com/37829.html
2-3. http://amzn.to/29LVX6v

Thursday, July 19, 2007[1]

you were wondering, weren't you?

So, another book after a long delay. I usually have 3 books being juggled between various spots and briefcases, and sometimes, like the previous three books, they all synch up to get finished at pretty much the same time, meaning that I'm *starting* three new ones all at once, leading to a reasonably long gap between reviews.

Anyway, after nearly a 2-week hiatus, another one bites the dust, as it were. This, Sacred Journeys: An Illustrated Guide to Pilgrimages Around the World[2] by Jennifer Westwood is a bit of an odd duck, which is likely the reason that I found it at the dollar store a few years back. I'm sure that this looked like a *lovely* project when the author and her friends were thinking it up, but unless you're *really into* pilgrimages, it's a strange read.

The book *is* about pilgrimage as a concept, as a literary thread, and as a travel modality. The main body of the book is set up in chapters which discuss the "stages" that one would go through were one to be going on a pilgrimage, in 12 chapters from "Longing" to "Coming Home". Each chapter also includes one to three 2-page "interludes" discussing a particular pilgrimage, written by somebody connected to that region. These 25 stories do not seem to be specifically keyed to the "stage" at hand, so have the feeling of having been randomly "tossed" into the book, and, frankly, make reading through it a bit jumpy. I ended up settling on a system of reading the "inserts" first, then the chapter, then moving to the next "inserts". The book also has a *second* part "A Guide To Sacred Places" which has brief over-views to an additional 40 pilgrimage sites, followed by a "Resources" section which provides contact and basic visiting information for many of the sites covered.

One gets that the author has been to a whole lot of interesting places (having traveled through Iran, etc., when that region was still exhibiting some sort of sanity), and would dearly like to go visit even more. Again, as various bits and pieces are pulled from other contributors, it's never crystal clear who is relating their travel experiences as one moves through the book. By the end, I was a bit tired of hearing of yet another "Mary" shrine, but I guess that's what one finds in Europe (Westwood *is* British). There were some major Buddhist shrines, however, that I was surprised that I had not heard of, so it wasn't all slanted to the Xtian mythos!

The availability on Sacred Journeys[3] seems a bit confusing. The large-format hardcover edition I have (from Holt) seems to be out of print, but available for under a buck for a "good" copy, and a bit over three bucks for a "like new" copy via the Amazon new/used guys. There is *another* hardcover edition also listed (for $35 new, $10 used), which does seem to still be in print, so this *might* be available via your local book vendor. Frankly, I'd go with the used on the big one if this sounds like something you'd want to get.

Notes:
1. http://btripp-books.livejournal.com/38046.html
2-3. http://amzn.to/29XXEh3

Monday, July 23, 2007[1]

A very good over-view ...

A lot of the books I read are, frankly, something of a "slog", the reading of which is much more a means to an end (of getting the data from the pages into my head) than a pleasurable experience. This was quite a nice departure from that modality. John Shirley's Gurdjieff: An Introduction to His Life and Ideas[2] was an engaging read, which I kept wanting to find time to get back into ... sort of like how fiction readers (and it's been over 3 years and nearly 140 books since I've read any fiction!) say they can't put a book down.

Perhaps the key of the attraction of this book is that the author appears to have been somebody who had encountered (and independently studied) the work of Gurdjieff and not a "follower" of any of the various 4th Way lineages, and had embarked on this book as a way of clarifying the man and his teachings primarily for his own personal edification ... a stance that I can, obviously, relate to, having read a couple of dozen books by or about G.I. Gurdjieff and P.D. Ouspensky, but never having any encounter with their surviving schools.

Shirley's Gurdjieff[3] is primarily a history, taking a "non-mythologized" look at the where/what/when of Gurdjieff's life, something which is difficult to track via the canonical materials. The author peels back the veils and tries to place the biographical bits into a literal context of the times, from the influences on the young Gurdjieff, to his "search for Truth" and his inner circle, and how that ebbed and flowed through the chaos of the Russian Revolution, and into the start of his "Institute for the Harmonious Development of Man", his interfacing with then alienating Ouspensky, and the eventual production of the books which put forth the "Fourth Way" teachings. As noted, I've read a goodly amount on the subject, but this book puts the whole "Gurdjieff group" in clearer context than I can recall seeing it, with a clear sense of who did what, where, and when (with juicy tidbits like when he told Aleister Crowley to "go and never come back" when the famed occultist made an uninvited visit to the Institute in 1926).

One of the most "useful" bits here is Shirley's "wiseacre interpretation" of the very difficult *Beelzebub's Tales To His Grandson*, taking the tortured (albeit carefully crafted) prose and wringing out from it some core ideas. Gurdjieff was fond of inventing ridiculously convoluted names for things discussed in *Beelzebub's*, and of endlessly on-running sentences. A.R. Orage spent *years* working with Gurdjieff to wrest an English version out of the Russian and Armenian manuscript, and Shirley's glosses on this are *very* welcome (I wish he'd do a interpretation of the whole 3-volume 1,200-page book!).

Also useful is the appendix which discusses "Bibliographical Suggestions" both of the Gurdjieff/Ouspensky canon (these will be forever linked by Ouspensky's *In Search of the Miraculous* which expresses Gurdjieff's teachings in a way that eventually healed the rift between them), and of books by and about their various followers.

I was reminded in reading bits of this (including another appendix about the "food for the moon" concept) of how some of Carlos Castaneda's critics have claimed that much of Castaneda's "system" was in many ways cribbed from Gurdjieff's ... the latter put out as plainly as Shirley does here allows for those very interesting parallels to be more evident than they might otherwise appear!

Needless to say, I highly recommend Gurdjieff: An Introduction to His Life and Ideas[4] ... and it does still appear to be in print, so could be found at your local brick-and-mortar bookseller. However, Amazon has it at 25% off of cover, and you can get a "new" copy from the new/used vendors for under five bucks (plus shipping). If you have any interest of learning about Gurdjieff and his teachings (or wouldn't mind having a fresh look), do pick up a copy of this!

Notes:

1. http://btripp-books.livejournal.com/38374.html

2-4. http://amzn.to/29K9cS8

Wednesday, July 25, 2007[1]

Another good one ...

Wow, two "can't put down" books in a row. Frankly, I didn't *start* on this one until I was done with that Gurdjieff book I reviewed a couple of days ago, and here I am with this one done already! Of course, I love archaeology, am interested in history, and am always open to heretical ideas, and this has all those woven together into a fascinating whole.

James D. Tabor's The Jesus Dynasty: The Hidden History of Jesus, His Royal Family, and the Birth of Christianity[2] starts out as an archaeological investigation. The author is the head of the Religious Studies Department at UNC-Charlotte with PhD from University of Chicago, and spends a lot of time in Israel supervising digs. The book begins with the accidental discovery of a couple of tombs, with some very interesting "clusters" of names, and then moves on to the earlier discovery of the "James, brother of Jesus" ossuary (a box for bones), and a discussion of 1st Century CE burial customs (yes, I *do* find this stuff fascinating). The book then shifts to a discussion of the general historical setting of the time, and eventually moves towards looking at the major players in the Jewish "Messianic" movement.

Much of the reality of early Christianity was "swept under the rug" by the later Church, and the bulk of The Jesus Dynasty[3] is spent uncovering the traces of Jesus' original teachings, using archaeological, historical, and textual sources. Much of this would not have been possible prior to the past few decades, but major discoveries have been made of "lost books", and computer analysis is able to separate out later over-lays on the early documentation.

The picture which emerges is of a "Nazarean" movement of certain families of Royal lineage. John (the Baptist) as the "High Priest Messiah" through descent from Aaron, and Jesus as the "King Messiah" through his mother's lineage back to David. Much is also covered on Jesus' paternity, of how likely Mary, betrothed to much older Joseph, had become pregnant, possibly by a Roman soldier named Pantera (cue *"Revolution Is My Name"*?), has Jesus in less than optimal circumstances, re-marries one of Joseph's brothers (as was common practice at the time) after his death, and has four additional sons and two daughters. These details are important following Jesus' execution in 30ce, as first James takes over the lineage, followed by Simon after James is executed in 62ce, followed by Jude once Simon is eliminated by the Romans in 106ce.

Most of this history is likely unfamiliar to mainstream Christians, as by the time the New Testament was being codified, the "mystical" Church of Paul (based solely on his hallucinations) had swept to prominence in Rome and its empire. Nearly all canonical traces of James and the "Jewish Christianity" were expunged, surviving only in echoes of the "Q document", extrapolated from the "non-Mark" parts of Matthew and Luke, and supported by surviving non-canonical sources such as the Greek *Didache*, and descriptive traces of pockets of authenticity such as the Ebionites. There were two reasons for this, the obvious one being that the "Pauline Church" wanted to play down the Church of Jesus and his lineage as much as possible as Paul's teachings bore little resemblance to Jesus', yet was anchored on his personage; second, the major Jewish revolts in 66-70ce (resulting in the destruction of the Temple and much of Jerusalem) and 132-135ce had polarized the Roman world against the now-destroyed Jewish civilization, and the Gentile Church was eager to keep it's "Jewish roots" out of sight as much as possible.

Needless to say, this is another major look at how what we know as "Christianity" would have been seen as the basest blasphemy by Jesus and those with whom he lived and worked. The co-opting of the Church of John, Jesus, and James by the "false prophet" Paul is perhaps the cruelest perversion of any religious movement in all of human history. I suppose it would be too much to hope that with the on-going discoveries of texts and archaeological evidence that the abomination that is Pauline Christianity could begin to be taken down from it's ill-gotten prominence!

Anyway ... I don't suppose I have to say that I *highly recommend* this book!

The Jesus Dynasty[4] is still in print (it only came out last year) in both hardcover and paperback, so could likely be found at your local bookstore. It's also at a discount via Amazon, and can be had in "good" copies of the hardcover for as little as $1.98 (plus shipping) via the new/used vendors over there. Whichever way you pick this up, DO pick it up and give it a read ... and hopefully start to *wake up* from the 2,000-year lie!

Notes:

1. http://btripp-books.livejournal.com/38426.html

2-4. http://amzn.to/29PUqwW

Friday, August 3, 2007[1]

How ironic ...

It seems somewhat "bittersweet" to have just finished this book before the current round of interviews which look like they might be leading me back *into* a "real job" after 15 years of being in the entrepreneurial wastelands. (sigh) Needless to say, I'm *torn* on the subject (but will be very happy to have some money coming *in* for a change!).

Anyway, I found Ernie Zelinski's Real Success Without a Real Job: There Is No Life Like It![2] very interesting, if a bit frustrating. Interesting in that it's a *great* "coaching" book for those looking to *escape* from "the corporate world", but frustrating in that I've tried so many of the things he writes about, and have (evidently) failed every time, leading me to my current desperate search for a "real job".

Frankly, it's somewhat hard for me to write a meaningful "review" of this, as Zelinski is, in my case, "preaching to the choir", as I don't need much *convincing* about the allure of the "unreal job", it's just that I've not has the success that I would hope for in that pursuit. I am, however, still *trying* to find a way to make that eventually happen, and he does have some pointed bits on how to structure your time, etc. to make this a reality.

Of course, Zelinski's main "case study" is his own story, which involves having been a very unhappy engineer who got down-sized from a job he hated, and deciding to write (and self publish/promote) books. This reminded me a bit of that "careers for New Agers" book[3] that I read a couple of months back ... whose author likewise specialized in cranking out books for a living. I, unfortunately, have always been of the Dorothy Parker mold when it comes to writing (her arch quote, which got stuck in my head via Truman Capote's frequent recitation of it, is "I enjoy having written", implying that the process of *writing* itself is less than pleasurable), and so require either some concrete goal or externally imposed discipline to attain to anything more expansive than these blog posts! Admittedly, to that end, Zelinski recommends *his* schedule of writing for 3 hours a day, and only expecting a result of 4 pages from that effort (to my credit, most of these reviews take less than an hour to write and are a full Word page at 10pt, a page and a half at 12pt, and two "book pages" generally, so the time-to-volume of text equation is not far off).

This is not to say that Real Success Without a Real Job[4] is all about writing as a career. He also provides stories of situations like "the guy who sold the Brooklyn Bridge" (having bought the "junk wood" from when the surface was upgraded and sold it a few inches at a time via mail order to make a fortune), and provides a list of a hundred "unreal jobs" (which, frankly, are not that unusual, mainly being a list of jobs one can have on a freelance or consultant basis, although including some not-top-of-mind career paths such as "busker", "stuntman", and "mime"). The book's strength, however, is in encouraging one to *consider* the "unreal" job while providing information on where to get specific additional information (such as a directory of "affiliate programs" for developing multiple income streams for one's web pages). Frankly, I ended up sticking in nearly a dozen bookmarks in this as I read it to allow me to go back and look up various of these resources!

Zelinski's book is fairly recent (so the data in it hasn't gotten "cold" yet), and is no doubt available at your local brick-and-mortar book vendor. Amazon has it at about 1/3rd off, which (if you combine stuff to bring the total up to free shipping) is pretty much a wash with the lowest of the "new/used" guys' pricing (with shipping). If you have an itch to get out of a current work rut and do something on your own, this could be a very useful book. Its only weakness is that it won't take you by the hand and detail a "what" that you should be doing, and lead you through the "how" involved ... but it does provide leads to at least get you started on your own "legwork".

Notes:

1. http://btripp-books.livejournal.com/38706.html
2. http://amzn.to/29IGx1B
3. http://btripp-books.livejournal.com/35426.html
4. http://amzn.to/29IGx1B

Saturday, August 11, 2007[1]

Big Math ... Weird Science ...

Yes, I'd read some reviews of Leonard Susskind's The Cosmic Landscape: String Theory and the Illusion of Intelligent Design[2] before I picked it up, and was wondering about how I'd like it. These were generally positive, but with caveats ... however, a good friend highly recommended it, so I got a copy and sorted it into the reading rotation. My over-all take on this is "it's not as good as it could have been" ... but failed in ways that are perfectly understandable.

Frankly, Susskind started to "lose" me about 2/3rds of the way through this, not through disinterest, mind you, but in my being able to retain and contextify the info he was expounding. Given that I've read (comparably to most readers) a *lot* of physics, and especially "cosmological" stuff like this, the fact that I was getting lost in this is rather telling. He does a *great job* up front in the book discussing QED, QCD, Feynman diagrams, Planck limits, the Cosmological Constant, and various spatial geometries, all leading up to the "Landscape" concept. However, at some point in there the explanations started to fade a bit and there would end up with lines like this:

> "... branes annihilated one another and rearranged, fluxes shifted, and the sizes and shapes of several hundred moduli changed ..."

Ouch. Again, I've read *a lot* of stuff in this genre, and a substantial part of the latter part of this book was "new" to me ... which, admittedly, is likely to be the cause of much of my head-scratching. At several points I'd wished that I was in the classroom so I could have raised a hand to get clarification e.g. *"Prof. Susskind, if there's a quark at one end of a string and an antiquark at the other, wouldn't there be a temporal frame when they'd cancel each other out?"* (given that the anti particles can be described as regular particles moving backwards in time).

I suspect that, were I in that classroom, my hand would be up frequently, asking for clarification on stuff like fluxes moving through the holes in toroidal geometries, the whole concept of strings terminating in D-branes (which can't help to infect one with a Cypress Hill "earworm"), and lovely things like the Calabi Yau Manifold (pictured here[3]), which are serious challenges to wrap one's mind around!

The whole thrust of the book is, of course, to place the Anthropic Principle (which basically says that the Universe is the way it is because if it was otherwise we would not be here to observe it) in a mathematically rigorous context which would serve as a bulwark against the "intelligent design" mob. Admittedly, there are things in the way the Universe is set up that are *highly* unlikely, but without them being right around that particular value, life as we know it would never have arose (the key of these, within the book, is the Cosmological Constant which is, for the first 119 decimal places, exactly zero, and only hitting a value, 1, at the 120th position, giving a value of 10^{-120}, which, in effect, becomes the "odds" of a Universe having us around to look at it). Now, the "Landscape" is not a *place* (as opposed to the *Megaverse*), but a mathematical description of "all possible Universes" in which there are "valleys" (pockets of stability) which detail the specific moduli of charge, spin, field strength, etc., etc., etc., including stuff like how big the Cosmological Constant will be. Now, 10^{-120} is a *very* small number, but according to Susskind's model, the Landscape encompasses 10^{500} "valleys", and 10^{500} is a nearly inconceivably large number (to put this in context, the current understanding of the *radius* of the observable Universe is 4.4 x 10^{26} meters, and the size of the "Planck Length", the smallest theoretical measure of space, is 1.6 x 10^{-35} meter, making the entire universe only something like 10^{50} Planck Lengths end-to-end ... the number of "valleys" is still 10^{450} times as many as that!). Needless to say, in a "Landscape" of that size, there are *plenty* of opportunities for a "life-friendly" Universe to arise ... and, yes, in the *Megaverse* there are nearly endless numbers of Universes arising, disappearing, expanding, contracting, and hosting curious apes like ourselves.

Anyway, with the caveats noted, I enjoyed the challenge of The Cosmic Landscape[4], although I'm disappointed in myself that I didn't "get" all the details (in my defense, I will note that I have not "formally" studied any math past pre-calc in 11th grade, so I'm doing pretty well when I'm getting the gist of stuff like this[5], and am not going to "beat myself up" for not following the likes of this[6]). As is usually the case on recent releases (this came out in 2005), it is both available at retail, and is not at "give away" prices via the new/used vendors ... although you *can* get a "new" copy of the hardback (with shipping) from those guys for just slightly less than Amazon is selling the paperback (pre-shipping). Hey, if you like stretching your brain (not "brane") out a bit with advanced math and hard-to-visualize physics theories, this might be the book for you!

Notes:

1. http://btripp-books.livejournal.com/39003.html
2. http://amzn.to/29HKuBC
3. http://bit.ly/2eeJU1x
4. http://amzn.to/29HKuBC
5. http://bit.ly/2eeP9hM
6. http://bit.ly/2eJA0pc

Sunday, August 12, 2007[1]

Been meaning to read this one for a while ...

Well, I *finally* got a copy of Idries Shah's The Englishman's Handbook[2], the third book in his "English" trilogy (following up 1980's *Darkest England* and 1988's *The Natives Are Restless*). Being an Octagon book, this is painfully expensive at retail ($35 for a 222-page hardcover), and for a while seemed "unavailable", so was being offered at highly inflated prices on the used end of things. This was issued *quite* posthumously in 2000 (Shah died in 1996), which makes me wonder just how much of this Shah was directly responsible, and how much associates (or one of his writer offspring) had to do with its publication.

Shah's "England" books sought to turn the tables on the typical "observing foreign culture" modality by taking something of a field anthropologist stance to looking at the English. Shah, while Afghan by birth and heritage, was educated and spent most of his life in England, giving him are rather lucid perspective on the foibles of his adopted land. Each of the three books has taken a different angle (history, culture, mind-set), and this one focuses on how the English *think*.

Now, one has to understand that Shah held that the English, descendants of the Angles (of Anglo-Saxon fame), originated as a wandering tribe that emerged from the general area of Afghanistan sometime in the dark recesses of history, and managed to co-opt every culture and people that they ended up setting amidst (hence the top billing in "Anglo-Saxon" although this came to Britain from Saxony), eventually becoming "The English" despite whatever other cultural influences (Norman, Dane, Roman, Celt, etc.) were in the mix. Towards the end of explaining how this could be, Shah postulates an "Englishman's Handbook", or some secret store of knowledge of how to confuse and marginalize "foreigners", at home or abroad.

The Englishman's Handbook[3] is more a collection of odd vignettes from conversations, press reports, etc., than its predecessors, with only one "cute story" of a fictionalized character for illustration purposes. This, I'm sure, is due to the book having been largely assembled by "his estate" (the official author/copyright-holder) from snippets and notes they found in his files.

As noted in previous reviews of Octagon books, Shah is a *fascinating* character. Held by many to be the Sufi "Teacher of the Age", and by as many as a total poseur in early "eurotrash mode" (asiatrash?), who was brilliant in working a mystical con. I was fascinated to learn that Shah was likely the "Jack Bracelin" (he wrote under many pen names, but it's telling that the Gerald Gardner biography by Bracelin was published by Shah's Octagon Press) who was a beneficiary of Aleister Crowley's will. Shah was later to go on to be given J.G.Bennet's (noted follower of Gurdjieff and Ouspensky) school and retreat center, so if he *was* fooling people, he was certainly fooling a lot of the top names in the mystical/occult world in the 40's, 50's and 60's (which appears to have been *before* he began his career as a Sufi teacher)! One interesting point (if Shah did indeed pen the Gardner biography) is that there is a rather *nasty* (and somewhat out-of-context) bit in this book about Gardner ... of course, this *could be* from a posthumous pen and not Shah's.

Anyway, I got this through the Amazon new/used vendors, albeit for a *lot more* than I usually pay (but with Octagon's pricing, it's hard to get a "deal"). It does appear to be back in print, so you should be able to find it new. Frankly, I would not specifically recommend this book without the context of its predecessors, but the three of them together (with the caveat that this is the weakest of them, largely lacking Shah's arch wit) make for a fascinating read.

Notes:

1. http://btripp-books.livejournal.com/39297.html

2-3. http://amzn.to/29JKZyi

Monday, August 13, 2007[1]

I was hoping this would help!

Remember all those "positivity" and "law of attraction" books I read a few months back? Remember how I bitched that "if you weren't a Happy Person you were screwed", yet there was never *anything* in these books about *how* to move from being an unhappy person being ground down under the heel of a sadistic universe to being one of those fortunate few who could use "The Secret[2]" to their advantage? Well, when I saw David Niven, Ph.D.'s The 100 Simple Secrets of Happy People: What Scientists Have Learned and How You Can Use It[3], I thought that this might be the "training manual" ... after all, it had *scientists* (instead of discarnate spirit guides) involved!

Unfortunately, this isn't so much a "manual" as an interpretive digest of various studies which had results suggestive of their subjects' feelings of well-being. Each of the 100 sections has the same structure, a title like "Do Things You Are Good At", a few sentences explaining the concept of the title, a couple of paragraphs of a personal or societal vignette (like the one in the "Get A Good Night's Sleep" section that noted that productivity rose 3% on Tuesdays in the fall of 1998 in the North-East versus previous years, apparently due to Monday Night Football starting an hour earlier that season!), and very brief summary paragraph from some formal research study that carried the theme forward.

Most of these 100 "secrets" are pretty much no-brainers, like "Don't Blame Yourself" or "Exercise" or "Turn Off The TV", but others are probably not top-of-mind like "Your Goals Should Be Aligned With One Another", "Keep Pen And Paper Handy", or "Believe In Ultimate Justice", where the explanatory copy is useful. Each section is between 1 and 1½ pages, so this is a quick read, and as varied and non-preachy as it is, it's enjoyable. How useful, ultimately, it is for a "Grumpy Gus" like myself is debatable, but I figure that if I pick up a few pointers, who knows ... maybe next thing I'll be using *perfect belief* to manifest a huge Lotto prize win into my life! Hey, I *have a ticket*, it could happen!

The 100 Simple Secrets of Happy People[4] does seem to be out-of-print at the moment, but there are lots of used copies out there, with Amazon's new/used offerings ranging from a penny for a "good" copy to a buck for "like new". Frankly, I got this via a clearance sale at Barnes & Nobel's web site. It's not a bad book to have sitting around (a top-of-the-toilet classic?), so if you see it for cheap, go ahead an pick up a copy, it'll make you feel better, really!

Notes:
1. http://btripp-books.livejournal.com/39488.html
2. http://btripp-books.livejournal.com/33791.html
3-4. http://amzn.to/29HKUYE

Wednesday, August 29, 2007[1]

Arrgh ... so behind on these!

Those who follow my regular blog (as opposed to my book review blog), know that I have been in a bit of chaos lately, and was on the road, etc. for most of the past two weeks. I brought along 2 books that I was half done with and another to start when those were finished, and I am definitely feeling the pressing weight of having 3 unwritten reviews hanging over my head at this point!

Richard Dawkins' A Devil's Chaplain: Reflections on Hope, Lies, Science, and Love[2] was the first one of these I got through (finishing it on 8/16 in Billings, MT). This was my second of Dawkins' books, and it took me a while to "get into the flow" of this being a collection of 30-some articles, papers, letters, and presentations he'd written over the years, generally cobbled together into thematic sections (although not specifically those themes enumerated in the sub-title).

In many ways, A Devil's Chaplain[3] reminded me of Carl Sagan's The Demon-Haunted World[4]. It is largely a defense of science against "fuzzy thinking", especially as manifested by religion, although it also has a lot of side-issue stuff in it as well. Collections like this can be *superb* (being the best of the minor works of an author, collected and arranged into a coherent whole), but are more often flawed by organization, selection, and editorial laxness. Unfortunately, this is on the majority side of that equation, bogged down a bit with paeans to fallen comrades and similar diversions.

The meat of this book, however, is the part dealing with religion. Back in the 1970's Dawkins coined the term "meme" and in this he postulates that religion is a *disease* spread on a memetic level; in the introduction to his "The Infected Mind" section he writes:

> *To describe religions as mind viruses is sometimes interpreted as contemptuous or even hostile. It is both. I am often asked why I am so hostile to "organized religion". My first response is that I am not exactly friendly towards disorganized religion either. As a lover of truth, I am suspicious of strongly held beliefs that are unsupported by evidence: fairies, unicorns, werewolves, any of the infinite set of conceivable and unfalsifiable beliefs epitomized by Bertrand Russell's hypothetical china teapot orbiting the sun. The reason organized religion merits outright hostility is that, unlike belief in Russell's teapot, religion is powerful, influential, tax-exempt, and systematically passed on to children too young to defend themselves. Children are not compelled to spend their formative years memorizing loony books about teapots. Government-subsidized schools don't exclude children whose*

> *parents prefer the wrong shape of teapot. Teapot-believers don't stone teapot-unbelievers, teapot-apostates, teapot-heretics and teapot-blasphemers to death. Mothers don't warn their sons off marrying teapot-shiksas whose parents believe in three teapots rather than one. People who put the milk in first don't kneecap those who put the tea in first.*

Brilliant. However, even this section is a bit uneven, despite the *Viruses of the Mind* piece being well worth the entire book. There is fascinating material dealing with his own schooling, reactions to the "usual suspects" trotted out when puzzling questions are addressed, and even an atheistic "call to arms" penned in the wake of the 9/11 attacks. Needless to say, I am hoping that Dawkins' The God Delusion[5] (which I own but have not managed to read as yet) builds upon the gems here and (by being a full book on the one topic) avoids the problems inherent in this format.

Of course, over-all, these are *quibbles*. I very much enjoyed the book once I made peace with its editorial structure, and would recommend it to anybody of the "freethought" bent. This is still in print, so should be available at your local brick-and-mortar book vendor, but is also at Amazon at a 22% discount, and is available from their new/used guys for about half off.

Notes:

1. http://btripp-books.livejournal.com/39918.html
2-3. http://amzn.to/29HH4yM
4. http://btripp-books.livejournal.com/33163.html
5. http://btripp-books.livejournal.com/47525.html

Thursday, August 30, 2007[1]

And now to piss off the other half of my readers ...

I gotta tell you, it's really not a whole lot of fun being a politically Conservative but socially Libertarian person in the world today. It seems, from where I'm standing, that *everybody* is insane. The people who aren't actively in the cheering section for everything anti-American are likely to have an Invisible Friend which defines almost everything else they do, and the ones who are not suckered in by religion are as willing to believe Leftist lies and participate in the most inexcusable behavior based on delusional theory. Having twisted the panties of the first group with my rah-rah review of Mr. Dawkins' book, I'm now going to raise the blood pressure of the latter crowd with a similarly enthusiastic plug for a "right wing" title.

I hadn't been as familiar with Mona Charen as I have been, for example, with Ann Coulter, but I assume that is because Ann's always got her face on Fox, which I'll tune in for five minutes here and there while inhaling a sandwich out in the kitchen. I'd known the name, but it was one of those that I wasn't even sure on which side of the fence she was. Well, from reading Useful Idiots: How Liberals Got It Wrong in the Cold War and Still Blame America First[2] I'd say that she's as sharp as Ann, but willing to leave religion at home, and not as eager to "make trouble"!

I have frequently written how I *wish* that liberals would read some book or another that I had just gotten done with, just to *see* themselves in some other context, and I had that same desire cropping up again and again while reading this book. Charen starts this with the end of the Cold War and how the Left has been desperately trying to re-write history to make it look like they never were on the wrong side of it. Throwing harsh light on the lies, she uses extensive research to show the trend from the early days of support of the Soviets through blatant disregard of all Communist atrocities, and the constant refrain that "if it wasn't for (America's sins), none of (fill in the current bloodbath) would be happening". Millions of deaths at the hands of Stalin, Mao, Pol Pot, and their admirers are brushed away by the left with platitudes that make lingering racism and economic stratification in the U.S. seem like worse crimes.

Frankly, I should try to steer clear of books like Useful Idiots[3] as I *really do* try to maintain a certain equanimity in my life, and reading the tales of what can only be called treason by nearly half of the political spectrum riles me up. Don't get me wrong, I am *extremely* grateful that books like this are out there to shed light on the "emperor's new clothes"-like pass that the Left gets, but when I'm done reading something like this I end up so frustrated that people who, by all rights, should have been hung as traitors decades ago manage to have thriving careers in politics, the media, entertainment and academia with nobody even *asking* why they're still breathing!

Once again, I wish a LOT of people would read this ... I would, honestly, like to have liberals read this and give me their take on it ... although I suspect it would be the old *"oh, you're still seeing commies under the bed!"* feint. Now, this is still in print, and you can get it from your local bookstore for twenty-eight bucks, but why not take advantage of Amazon's new/used vendors ... there are currently *nine* copies of the hardcover edition for **1¢** (or an even $4 with shipping), ranging from "good" to "like new", available from those guys. Come on, *four* lousy bucks to have your eyes opened to the perfidy of the Left ... what's keeping your from looking?

By the way, this was another of the books finished on my recent long road trip, and I suspect that it will amuse some that this was finished on 8/20 when we were in Boise.

Notes:

1. http://btripp-books.livejournal.com/39941.html
2-3. http://amzn.to/29JIxYD

Friday, August 31, 2007[1]

An odd one ...

Every now and again I run across a book that makes me wonder just how it managed to find its way into print, and this was an example of that type. In many ways, this seems to be the author wanting to show off his hobby of making funny drawings ... but how does one convince a major publisher to come out with a large-format hardcover based on that desire? I suppose to have the author/artist being (to quote from the dust jacket) *"one of the twentieth century's great psychologists of perception and cognition"* who holds a chair at Stanford and has a long list of technical publications would help a lot at getting a "vanity" book out, but the suspicion that this *is* a "vanity" project hovers heavily over Roger N. Shepard's Mind Sights: Original Visual Illusions, Ambiguities, and Other Anomalies, With a Commentary on the Play of Mind in Perception and Art[2].

There is certainly enough *content* here to justify a book on the subject, but the fact that the examples always come back to the author's own sketches (when *other* examples from art and advertising might have better illustrated the points being made) drags the book away from achieving its goals. Of course, this is also described (again from the dust jacket) as *"part autobiography, part artists' portfolio"*, so I guess the "see how clever I am" (also carried into the text, with stories of "pranks" by the author, such as arranging for his daughter to publish a paper on a subject that he had previously published, partnered with a researcher having the same last name as his co-publisher, so that there would be *two* papers on the same subject by the same last-name researchers, just a few decades apart ... ensuring, no doubt, that hilarity would ensue) theme is actually more the point than the putative subject itself.

Mind Sights[3] is in three sections, the first discussing "visual tricks" in general, and the author's life story, a section devoted to reproducing various drawings, broken into thematic groups, and, finally, an analysis of what is going on psychologically in the perception of the "tricks" involved. Needless to say, this last bit is the "meat" of the book but one needs to plow through a whole lot of Jack Horner-esqe *"what a ~~good~~ smart boy am I!"* posturing to get there.

Now, this is one of those books that has been languishing in my to-be-read boxes for a long time (selected to be easy to finish up on my recent road trip), and is currently out-of-print, so were you *dying* to find out what a bright and creative fellow Mr. Shepard is, you'll have to make some extra effort than dropping by your local bookstore. New/used copies are available, but not for particularly cheap, the lowest is currently $2.78 (plus shipping, of course) for a "good" copy of the paperback edition, but you can have a "like new" copy of the hardcover for only $7.99 which, considering this came out at $24.95 in 1990, isn't a bad deal ... were you interested in this, that is.

Oh, and for those of you keeping track of my "review backlog", this is the last of the books finished up on the road trip, and I got done with this one in the five hour delay we endured sitting on some distant patch of tarmac at the Indianapolis airport waiting to find some way to return to (tornado-harried) Chicago last Thursday (8/23).

Notes:

1. http://btripp-books.livejournal.com/40234.html

2-3. http://amzn.to/29HFKvX

Sunday, September 9, 2007[1]

A good read ...

As those who have been following along in my regular journal know, we are currently faced with the prospect of moving from Chicago and off to the wilds of the "mountain north-west". One of my (many) concerns out that way is running into a far more "religiously polarized" environment than I have ever had to deal with (being that I have, with the exception of my college years, only lived in downtown Chicago and New York City). Aside from researching UU groups in the various cities we're considering, I recently got a bunch of "humanist" books for my daughters, and Dale McGowan's Parenting Beyond Belief: On Raising Ethical, Caring Kids Without Religion[2] for me.

As those of you have followed my reading over the past couple of years will know, it's rare that I read anything that hasn't been sitting around for a while, so this, which was just published earlier this year, is quite "fresh". The book is a collection of essays around 9 general topic areas, from personal stories, how to "frame" religion and science, and the on to the basic stuff like holidays, death, and community. Dale McGowan is the editor and contributed four out of the forty pieces here, as well as each section's introduction and the various "additional resources" info. Now, I frequently have issues with "collections" like this, due to the unavoidable shift in writing style piece-to-piece, but because of the *thematic* consistency it holds together better than many books of this type, although there are certainly contributors that you would prefer not to get into a long read with!

I wonder if McGowan had set out to have some "celebrity" flash to this, or if that was his publisher's idea, as, frankly, I felt that inclusion of Julia Sweeny, Penn Jillette, and Richard Dawkins, while being on-theme, were simply there to splash their names on the cover (all three are in the "Personal Reflections" section at the start of the book, so don't have an "essential" role for any given "subject" portion of the book, and all three pieces are, I believe, available elsewhere). Of course, Penn Jillette perhaps has the most "like me" stance in the book, here's a sweet bit from his all-too-brief contribution:

> We don't have any friends who are into any kind of faith-based hooey, so our kids will just think that "damn it" follows "god" like "Hubbard" (or something) follows "mother".

Heh, heh, heh ... no, we didn't start out to ensure The Girls swore like longshoremen either.

Anyway, Parenting Beyond Belief[3] is a very good book if you are looking for some way to insulate your kids from whatever Religious Insanity you might be having to deal with. As noted, it is very up-to-date, so the "additional resources" sections are just rife with good links and book recommendations on which to follow up.

Being that this a *new* book, you're not likely to get any break on the price ... but Amazon has it at 1/3rd off of cover, which makes it pretty reasonable, and it is no doubt available at your friendly neighborhood brick-and-mortar book monger as well. If you have kids and are creeped out by the Religion Zombies, this is a great book to pick up!

Notes:

1. http://btripp-books.livejournal.com/40484.html
2-3. http://amzn.to/1UpBya1

Monday, September 10, 2007[1]

More science ...

Those of you paying "stalking level" attention to my journal may recall that a while back I was enthused for having gotten a number of books from B&N's web site for two bucks a piece (I do so *love* a deal), and this was another of that bunch of books.

Frankly, I still don't quite "get" how/why Timothy Ferris' The Whole Shebang: A State-of-the-Universe(s) Report[2] ended up in that deep-discount category, unless there's a new edition out and they were clearing out the old ones (I'm just guessing in that Amazon lists the cover price on this as two bucks *more* than what's printed on the copy I have). It's obviously still in print, and the cover boasts it being a "national bestseller", so maybe I just lucked out!

I really need to improve my "bookmarking" for things like this, as I will end up with a half a dozen slips of paper stuck in a book, but then not really be sure what it was that I was trying to point out. Sometimes it's a fascinating fact, sometimes a particularly lush bit of prose, sometimes ... well, you get the picture. I know that *one* of my marks in this (in the endnotes) was to reflect on the factoid that Hugh Everett (the scientist who came up with, in his doctoral dissertation, the "many worlds" concept that every act of quantum measurement splits the universe into multiple copies, each reflecting the possible states of that measurement, and thus provided the time stamp of "pre- or post-Everett" discussions on the subject) ended up leaving "regular"" physics to work with *defense contractors* for a couple of decades, and was just about to "come back in from the cold" (as his theories had held up over time and he was finally being invited to seminars, etc.) and re-join the Theoretical Physics brotherhood when he had a sudden heart attack in 1982 and died. How about *that* for some conspiracy-theory fodder? Even more so, *just what military projects would have been benefiting from 25 years of his work?*

Anyway, aside from *that* little doozie, I don't recall specifically what I was wanting to bring up here to enlighten you on The Whole Shebang[3] other than one additional datum that, according to Ferris, there is, in the "observable universe" one supernova occurrence *per second*, which sure makes *me* want to buy a telescope ... oh, and an observation that when Ferris gets into the concept of "cosmic evolution" (yes, it does seem to be a bit convoluted), he postulates that *"Every evolutionary process has three aspects - one conservative, another innovative, and the third selective."* which could have been pulled directly from Gurdjieff's writings! I have no idea if Ferris has read any "Fourth Way" materials, but I sure get excited when stuff dovetails like this.

Over-all, The Whole Shebang[4] is "yet another Cosmology book" (of which I've probably read a dozen or more), so much of this was, for me, yet another look at stuff I've been familiar with for a while. To his credit, Ferris has *structured* this in a rather interesting and useful format, going from the Big

Bang, through the expansion, to a look at possible universal geometries, how all this relates to chemistry and the elements, what "dark matter" might be and why we're pretty sure 90% of the universe is made of it, how the universe may be structured, how what's in it has "evolved", a look at "symmetry", how the universe is growing, some of the concepts of this just being one of many universes, the whole "quantum weirdness" thing, a look at the assorted "anthropic" arguments, and even a theological coda.

As familiar as I am with much of this stuff at this point, there are always things in these books which surprise me, and this was no exception. In this case the most challenging bit was the work of Hartle and Hawking to try to devise a mathematical scenario that would avoid a singularity at the very beginning of everything, creating "world line" diagrams where the "vanishing point" singularity gets "smeared" and one is left with what looks like some badly mangled paperclips (trust me, it's *fascinating*, see p.253). Frankly, there was enough stuff flying around my head (ala Dennis Miller's "sub referencing"), that I was spinning out scenarios dealing with stuff (not covered in here) like String Theory's 11D space, and how that might explain/enable "action at a distance" questions in the cosmological models being covered in Ferris' text. I always appreciate a book that forces me to make diagrams!

If this sounds like your cup of tea, The Whole Shebang[5] is still in print, and should be available somewhere near you, but it *is* also out there for cheap … while the B&N sale from whence I got *my* copy is long gone, the Amazon new/used guys have at least one "like new" copy of the paperback for 1¢ and "like new" copies of the hardback for as little as a buck. Such a deal!

Notes:

1. http://btripp-books.livejournal.com/40867.html

2-5. http://amzn.to/29FGH7P

Tuesday, September 11, 2007[1]

Hmmmmm ...

A couple of weeks back I was enthusing about having found these "Dover Thrift Editions" on Amazon, and this is the first of that stack (I got 6 for me, 4 for Daughter #1, and one additional book for me that wasn't from Dover) that I've plowed through.

While these certainly are *thrifty*, they are also (for the most part) rather brief ... the text of Thoreau: A Book of Quotations[2] being a scant 60 pages. Edited by a Bob Blaisdell (who seems to have been involved in a number of these volumes), this collects 500 bits culled from Henry David Thoreau's writings, from the famous works like *Walden* and *Civil Disobedience* to thoughts lifted from his journal and personal letters, arranged thematically into 17 headings.

According to the editor, Thoreau *"is the most popular, and seemingly, least dated of America's nineteenth-century authors, as his voice and attitude often appear thoroughly modern"*, which seems to be the canonical "take" on him. Personally, I have always found this "modern" label oddly put on a man whose obsession of nature would seem to dismiss all that *is* modern. However, taken in the context of his time, many of his stances, to work, religion, and civil disobedience (which is noted as being an influence on the likes of Ghandi), are, perhaps *quite* modern indeed.

I assume that I read *some* Thoreau in my highschool and college years (I'm sure he's in that big two-volume set of English & American lit that was my frequent companion for much of that time), but it was never something that I enjoyed enough to either seek out independently or remember any more than vague impressions. As such, aside from the "famous lines" (ala *"The mass of men lead lives of quiet desperation."*), most of what has been assembled in Thoreau: A Book of Quotations[3] was new to me.

Predictably, I was most taken with Thoreau's quotes on Religion, as he seems to have been both well read in various faiths, and no fan of "priestcraft" (or, it would seem, "simple piety"). Having been a student of Ralph Waldo Emerson, much of his reflections in this area bear the marks of his teacher's transcendentalist leanings, although certainly framed in his own world-view. One quote that I found particularly, well, "modern" was:

> *"Do not be too moral. You may cheat yourself out of much life so. Aim above morality. Be not simply good; be good for something."*

Another quote that I found *fascinating* is a little snipped from *Walden* that would seem to presage one of Gurdjieff's trademark concepts: *"Moral reform is the effort to throw off sleep"* ... one has to wonder if the later mystic's "war against sleep" was at all informed by Thoreau's writings!

As one would expect from being in a "thrift" edition, this slim volume can be had for very little cash ... indeed the *cover price* on this is only $1.50! I inquired at my local brick-and-mortar book dealer about the availability of these and they indicated that they could be ordered, but must be pre-paid for in advance. Amazon, of course, has this and so your best bet, were you inclined to pick this up, would be to add this on one of those orders that is almost-but-not-quite up to the $25 free shipping threshold.

Notes:

1. http://btripp-books.livejournal.com/41069.html

2-3. http://amzn.to/29Gv9rk

Thursday, September 13, 2007[1]

Poetry ... not mine

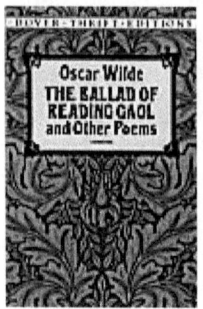

Oh, woe the English Major ... though all the uncountable hours of reading to find there is no market for thy skills! OK, so maybe it at least gives me a stance from which to bitch about stuff. *"Hi, my name's Brendan and I'm an English Major." ("Hi Brendan!")* Sometimes I think I'm *scarred* from the experience. I certainly "have issues" with various elements of literature; one of which is a love/hate relationship with poetry. I used to *write* poetry, enthusiastically even (at a pace of 250[2] poems a year, for quite a long time), and had started out (like pretty much everybody else) writing *rhymed* verse (I did sci-fi sonnet cycles, is that geeky enough for ya?), but came to generally dislike the all-too-limiting discipline of being locked into very narrow palates of words. Eventually, I discovered writers like the great John Ashbery[3] and found that poetry could be the literary equivalent of visual arts, restoring my love of the form.

This collection of the notorious Oscar Wilde's poetry, The Ballad of Reading Gaol and Other Poems[4], straddles the line of my love and hate of poetry. Frankly, to my ears (eyes), many of the "Other Poems" here are insufferable, largely due to lockstep short-line ABAB, ABBA, AABB, etc. with assorted CC additions. Things like:

> *All her bright golden hair*
> *Tarnished with rust,*
> *She that was young and fair*
> *Fallen to dust.*
>   - from "Requiescat"

... just make me *cringe*, and much of this slim volume floats into that zone ... from things like the above to poems where the first couple of lines of a stanza are truly evocative, only to fall apart as the poet stretches to find some words to fit the rhyme scheme, ala:

> *The Thames nocturne of blue and gold*
> *Changed to a Harmony in grey :*
> *A barge with ochre-colored hay*
> *Dropt from the wharf : and chill and cold*
>   - from "Impression du Matin"

{shudder} Frankly, as I paged into this, I was wondering if I was going to be able to force myself to *finish* it ... quite a damning thought for a book with a scant 50 pages of text! Fortunately, it appears that Mr. Wilde was at his best when taking up the challenge of a longer piece, and (as part of the challenge, I suppose) going to less generic rhyme schemes.

For example, the following. While, perhaps, if broken up differently, this would be less interesting, but in it he "buries" one rhymed word within a line and creates a weaving of sounds from what (were they to be brief lines with terminal rhymes) could be otherwise far less enticing ... exhibiting something of an (A)B/(B)A structure:

> *But these, thy lovers, are not dead. Still by the hundred-cubit gate*
> *Dog-faced Anubis sits in state with lotus-lilies for thy head.*
>
> *Still from his chair of porphyry gaunt Memnon strains his lidless eyes*
> *Across the empty land, and cries each yellow morning unto thee.*
>
> *And Nilus with his broken horn lies in his black and oozy bed*
> *And till thy coming will not spread his waters on the withering corn.*
> — from "The Sphinx"

Of course, as one would suspect, the best is getting top billing, and "The Ballad of Reading Gaol" is quite a haunting, stark, and gripping piece, While still *rhymed*, it takes on a somewhat liturgical A/B/C/B/D/B pattern (with additional, yet irregular, internal rhymes on the A, C, and D lines), suggesting call-and-response or the tolling of a bell.

> *He did not pass in purple pomp,*
> *Nor ride a moon-white steed.*
> *Three yards of cord and a sliding board*
> *Are all the gallows' need :*
> *So with rope of shame the Herald came*
> *To do the secret deed.*
>
> *We were as men who through a fen*
> *Of filthy darkness grope :*
> *We did not dare to breathe a prayer,*
> *Or to give our anguish scope :*
> *Something was dead in each of us,*
> *And what was dead was Hope.*
>
> *For Man's grim Justice goes its way,*
> *And will not swerve aside :*
> *It slays the weak, it slays the strong,*
> *It has a deadly stride :*
> *With iron heel it slays the strong,*
> *The monstrous parricide!*
> — from "The Ballad of Reading Gaol"

To quote Larry The Cable Guy: *"Now, that's good stuff there!"* ... however, as noted, this collection is (to my tastes, at least) quite uneven, yet, in the final analysis, the good outweighs the bad in <u>The Ballad of Reading Gaol and Other Poems</u>[5], and being that it's only a buck-fifty in the Dover Thrift Edition, you're not out much to get some really remarkable work! This is available (on order) from most stores, but it's one of those things that's probably best left to "add on" on your next on-line book shopping expedition.

Notes:
1. http://btripp-books.livejournal.com/41405.html
2. http://eschatonbooks.com/projects.html
3. http://www.poets.org/poet.php/prmPID/238
4-5. http://amzn.to/29FwMPY

Sunday, September 16, 2007[1]

Wow ...

This is *quite* a powerful book. It's the sort of thing that one would hope would be in the Social Studies curriculum of every highschool in the U.S., but I doubt that's going to happen. Dover Thrift Editions' Great Speeches by Native Americans[2], edited by Bob Blaisdell, costs a scant $2.50 *cover*, so it would be one of the *cheapest* texts to assign a class, but the sort of light this throws on our history is not likely to be welcome by many.

Now, as "regular readers" of this space may recall, I have read quite a number of "Native American" books, ranging from the Black Elk books on NA spirituality (and their like) to the more "political" books of Vine Deloria Jr.; originally being interested in filling in the North American gaps in my shamanic studies which have been primarily in South and Central America. Much of the "history from the *other* side" genre (which this book clearly is), also hits me in an uncomfortable place, as I have at least *two* Mayflower ancestors, so all of the Bad Things being done by Whites to the natives are pretty easily extrapolated as having a fair likelihood of being "crimes of my fathers", as we've been around here since 1620!

Great Speeches by Native Americans[3] covers a rather large chunk of time, the earliest speech in here dates from 1540 (addressing the ravages of the Spanish on the indigenous tribes of Florida), and the latest is from 1991 (a presentation at an Aboriginal Law Association conference) ... 450 years of pretty much saying *"We can't believe you Whites are being such total jerks!"*, as even in the non-confrontational pieces, the theme of broken promises and ignored treaties is a common thread.

Of course, I'd been familiarized with the general outline of the history here (from reading Deloria and others), but it does really bring it home to see Chief after Chief in decade after decade (the book is organized chronologically), voicing the same concerns, the same complaints, and (generally speaking) asking for the same redresses. It is notable, that *some* of these speakers had a better grasp on the situation that others, and, unfortunately, *those* were the ones strongly agitating for all-out armed response such as Tecumseh, who attempted to forge a unified front of native tribes to fight on the British side in the War of 1812:

> *"The White men are not friends to the Indians: at first they only asked for land sufficient for a wigwam; now, nothing will satisfy them but the whole of our hunting grounds, from the rising to the setting sun."*

It is interesting that there are countering speeches from other Chiefs included, who *clearly* did not "understand the situation" the way Tecumseh did, believing that if they were neutral, or sided against the British *"You can then return to your lands, and hunt the game, as you formerly did."*, arguing that to follow Tecumseh would mean obliteration (possibly true), but not taking into consideration the already long history of American expansion!

The quoted pieces come from a wide variety of sources (including the Congressional Record from official appearances of Chiefs in the capitol), and range from brief half-page snippets to extensive (20-30 page) works such as William Apes' 1836 "Eulogy on King Phillip". Another longish one is by Chief Joseph (of the Nez Percé) whose 1879 address in Washington D.C. outlined the recent history of his tribe, and how they had desperately tried to hold onto their traditional land. In the closing section of this he expresses his desires in a manner that should warm the heart of any Libertarian ...

> "Let me be a free man - free to travel, free to stop, free to work, free to trade where I choose, free to choose my own teachers, free to follow the religion of my fathers, free to think and talk and act for myself - and I will obey every law or submit to the penalty."

Powerful stuff. Frankly, I wonder if Crowley had a copy of this at hand when he penned Liber Oz[4] several decades[5] later, as the words (and desires) of Chief Joseph can certainly be seen to echo in the latter document.

Again, I really believe that Great Speeches by Native Americans[6] should be required reading of all Americans, just to understand that reaching our current place in the world "wasn't pretty" and has left a stain on our national character that we choose to ignore. As noted, this is in the Dover Thrift series, so is *remarkably* affordable at $2.50 ... and can be had via either your local brick-and-mortar bookstore or on-line (these are *great* for "nudging" a sub-$25 order up to free shipping). Do go pick up a copy of this, however ... it's a real eye-opener!

Notes:

1. http://btripp-books.livejournal.com/41671.html
2-3. http://amzn.to/29MjC7x
4. http://www.hermetic.com/crowley/libers/lib77.html
5. http://www.hermetic.com/sabazius/ozgloss.htm
6. http://amzn.to/29MjC7x

Thursday, September 20, 2007[1]

"Nietzsche, Nietzsche, Nietzsche!"

30 years ago I took a college class entitled "Irrationality", which an old German lady, Elizabeth Koffka (widow of gestalt psychologist Kurt), was, for some strange reason, auditing. She was a walking encyclopedia of (especially German) psychology and philosophy (much to the chagrin of our instructor), and would often regale us with various remembrances. The title of this posting is one wag's joke about what she'd say while tickling a baby ... *"Nietzsche, Nietzsche, Nietzsche!"*. Unfortunately, this was about as close to reading Nietzsche as I got during my college career.

As such, my recently picking up Friedrich Nietzsche's The Genealogy of Morals[2] was to make some attempt to fill in a particular intellectual gap from my college years. While I triple majored, and have read a vast deal in the ensuing decades, my grounding in "philosophy" is decidedly second or third hand for the most part. I have never much been drawn to philosophy as an area of study, and I think in reading this book I have come to some understanding of why.

Frankly, I can pick up the "broad strokes" of obscure physics theories in a reasonably-attentioned read of a well written book on the subject, and the same is true for most arcane religious texts. What I found in reading Nietzsche was that one is almost forced into reading and re-reading to "get" what is being *meant*. The Genealogy of Morals[3] is a collection of three themed papers, with 17, 25, and 28 sections respectively, and it struck me as I was going through this that it would be more productive to have a small study group approaching this section by section, and then discussing each in turn. To be honest, unless one has an extreme aptitude for navel-gazing, this is more time out of one's life than I am willing to dedicate to it, having "places to know, people to be" (or something like that).

The three papers deal with "Good and Evil", "Guilt" and the "Ascetic Ideal", each grinding through Western (mainly, although aspects of Eastern thought do come into play, for instance where he attributes India the distinction of having the most "philosophic ability" and England the least) civilization as something of a battle between "master" and "slave" mentalities, with the former being more of the pre-Christian cultures and the latter the institutionalized cult of suffering, creating a world as an *"ascetic planet, a den of discontented, arrogant, and repulsive creatures who never got rid of a deep disgust of themselves, of the world, of all life, and did themselves as much hurt as possible out of pleasure in hurting - presumably their one and only pleasure"*.

Almost more fascinating that the book is the brief biographical sketch that serves as its introduction, bringing all sorts of interesting facts to light (including how much of Nietzsche's "proto-Nazi" image came from his extremely anti-Semitic sister who took him in and managed his affairs during the mental decline of his last years) ... I suspect that I would have preferred reading a good *biography* of the man more than this one slice of his *ideas*. Of course, this is an issue of personal preference, I don't mean to dismiss the book, which (while hardly being a "fun read") was very interesting within its context. I guess I'm just not a "philosophy guy".

Anyway, this is another of those remarkable Dover Thrift Edition books, and has a cover price of a scant $3.00 ... which makes it an easy addition to one's library if one is inclined, as I was, to make the effort to add some Nietzsche to one's "mental mix". As noted on previous titles, these are available via brick-and-mortar vendors, but will likely need to be ordered (why stock the $3 Dover edition when you can stock somebody else's $9 version?). Again, keeping these "at the ready" as an add-on to order via Amazon, etc. is probably the best bet for times when one might be contemplating placing an order that would otherwise be just shy of the $25 free shipping level.

Notes:

1. http://btripp-books.livejournal.com/41951.html

2-3. http://amzn.to/29zRLVA

Monday, September 24, 2007[1]

As if this needs an introduction ...

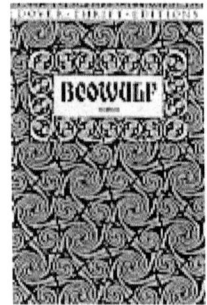

So, *of course* I've read Beowulf[2] before. It seems like *everybody* has. On LibraryThing[3] it would be the 95th most popular book if it wasn't for J.K. Rowling, but I assume that this is from a lot of basic highschool and college English courses requiring it and not a factor of raw popularity. Frankly, I'm surprised that I don't already have a couple of copies in my logged-in library, as I *recall* a couple of different versions from school, but they must have gone "elsewhere" at some point.

I picked up this the other day when I was ordering a bunch of the Dover Thrift Editions books because it seemed to be a good lead-in to another book I was getting, and it was all of a whopping $1.50 addition to the order. Unfortunately, the Dover edition of Beowulf[4], translated by R. K. Gordon, is probably less "accessible" than other versions that I remember, as it neither attempts to render the Old English into modern English verse (as many do), nor does it try to create a modern narrative of the story, rather this seems to attempt providing the "feel" of the Old English, which makes following the tale a bit of a challenge.

Beowulf[5] was set down in Old English sometime around 1000 ce, although the story it tells dates to as early as 500 ce and deals with figures from the Danish, Swedish, and Geat (part of modern Sweden) kingdoms. One of the reasons that this book has the attention that it does is that it is a rare example of an early surviving text in a "European vernacular", and it also preserves a "pure" Germanic English linguistic thread, soon to be muddled via the Norman invasion of England in the century after this was set down.

One of the challenges of coming to a "not excessively annotated" version of Beowulf[6] is that, to the initial audience for this story, it was a familiar tale from an already "mythic" age, and so a lot of the "back story" of the characters (and their assorted inter-relations) would have been already familiar from an oral tradition; where, to the modern reader, it's just a lot of very odd names (Healfdene, Hrothgar, Hygelac, Ecgtheow, Ongentheow, Eadgila, etc., etc., etc.) who live in hard-to-pronounce places (well, aside from Denmark and Sweden), doing stuff that was at times sort of hard to figure out. An example:

> Weohstan slew him in battle with the edge of the sword, a friendless exile, and bore off from his kin the bright gleaming helm, the ringed corselet, the gigantic old sword that Onela gave him, his kinsman's war-trappings, ready battle equipment.

Yeah, picking through in context you can eventually get what's going on (the one guy killed the other guy and took all his good stuff), but it requires a good deal of re-reading to stay caught up!

Needless to say, I'm torn on this point. While it's "special" to have the "feel" of the Old English original, it does make *reading* it a bit of a chore, but it brings an antiquity to the experience ... on the other hand, a more modern version would provide the details of the action, but would lack that "oldness". Of course, there are dozens of versions of this book, there are something like fifty different covers on its LibraryThing[7] page, so there are more than enough to choose from!

Again, I picked up the Dover Thrift Edition "because it was there (for a buck and a half)" and fit into some of my current reading ... as Dennis Miller says: "your mileage may vary". However, if you're one of those non-Liberal Arts types and feel that your education in medieval epics is lacking, here's an inexpensive way to fill in those gaps! As noted in previous postings, while these *are* in print, you local store is unlikely to be carrying them, but you can order them ... but all the better to have a buck-fifty title like this ready to go the next time your Amazon or B&N order is hovering just south of free shipping.

Notes:

1. http://btripp-books.livejournal.com/42235.html
2. http://amzn.to/29yv4V2
3. http://btripp-books.com/
4-6. http://amzn.to/29yv4V2
7. http://btripp-books.com/

Wednesday, September 26, 2007[1]

Lots of pictures ...

Well, *this* was a fast read! Chicago Then And Now[2] by Elizabeth McNulty was part of my birthday haul over the weekend. I am a real sucker for historic photos of my town, so I dove right into this, and had gotten through the book before my actual birthday was half over. Of course, there is only a smattering of text in this, most of the book being an old photo and a new photo of the same building, neighborhood, or view on facing pages, with a couple of describing paragraphs.

It was especially cool to see several pages shot in my neighborhood, with our building in the background of one of them. I was surprised to find several factoids which were in the "I *did not* know that" category, like seeing Grant Park barely laid out with no trees (but with some very recognizable features) in 1929, or reading that Chicago was supposed to have *five* "municipal piers", of which Navy Pier (which was officially #2) was the only one built. Also surprising was how many very recognizable (and still extant) buildings can be pointed out in an 1936 aerial view ... and several familiar blocks where everything survives from the 1890's ... and that two main buildings in a shot from Chinatown in 1928 are still standing (one housing our favorite Dim Sum place!). Also odd to consider are shots from the south Loop before there *was* "the loop" ... the El being such a defining element to Chicago's downtown ... but here are pictures from 1895 showing decorative fronts of buildings that have been obscured by tracks for more than a century.

I was slightly miffed to find some tell-tale photoshopping (careless photoshopping at that) in at least one "now" picture ... you would think that if they were going to mess with some of these they might have taken out some "melt" spots on the antique negatives and not have left a duplicated sign edge hanging over Milwaukee Avenue in a modern shot!

Needless to say, this is a book for fans of either antique photos, urban history, or da grate city of Chicago. Since I'm pretty much all three, it was a home run for me, but I'm pretty sure this isn't *everybody's* cup of tea. Being a hardcover picture book, it's not cheap, but it's not unreasonable either, and "new" copies can be had via the Amazon new/used guys for eight something before shipping.

Notes:

1. http://btripp-books.livejournal.com/42274.html
2. http://amzn.to/29Ft4pw

Sunday, September 30, 2007[1]

Spoiler Alert!

Alrighty then ... *damn near everybody dies horribly* ... OK, you can come back to reading now!

Yes, this is The Nibelungenlied[2] (in D.G. Mowatt's prose translation), the source material for Wagner's 4-opera, 14-hour *Der Ring des Nibelungen* cycle. I, like most folks, have been exposed to snippets of this over the years but have not sat through even *one* of the operas complete, let alone the entire cycle (various versions of which *are* available on DVD from Amazon). As such, I was generally familiar with some of the characters, and a few bits of the action, but at a sufficient distance that most of this was "fresh" in reading.

I had planned to have knocked down this back-to-back with *Beowulf*, as this was penned in Middle High German a few centuries past that, but likewise looking back towards a semi-mythical time around the fifth century. I don't know if it is the source material or the translation, but The Nibelungenlied[3] was a far more "accessible" read in that it is *much* easier to follow the characters and action in this.

However, I kept finding myself thinking of less-than-flattering modern parallels to what was happening in the book. The first third or so was pretty much "soap opera with some fantastic elements", sort of like Dark Shadows[4] but without the vampires, the second third or so was a lot like the Rambo movies, with a few key warriors killing hundreds if not thousands of enemies without incurring much damage themselves, and a finish that was, *so bloody* that it brought to mind the classic Monty Python *Sam Peckinpah's "Salad Days"* sketch[5]. All of this set in a context of "courtly" behavior and exchanged obligations that, by the end, make the web of alliances that got the first World War started seem rational (frankly, one of the "best parts" in this is the long exchange between Rüdeger and the Burgundians in which both sides are anguishing over not wanting to fight each other, which greatly echoes Arjuna's angst at Kurukshetra, making me wonder if the much older Indian epic, *Mahabharata* had somehow managed to influence this story).

While the characters of The Nibelungenlied[6] are familiar to modern folks via Wagner's works, it was surprising how little of the Germanic/Norse mythology appears in this. While there are Dwarfs, Giants, magic cloaks of invisibility, Dragons, etc., etc., etc., there are no appearances of Wotan, Valhalla, Yggdrasil, the Norns (although an analogous, if minor, scene is in this), Valkyries, etc., and a *central* character to this story, Kriemhilde (sister to Gunther, wife, and eventual avenger, of Sifrid) is left out of the operas!

One thing I found interesting was how wide-spread (for the 5th century) the locations were ... there were folks from Iceland, Denmark, Burgundy, Verona, Hungary, the Netherlands, and mentions of others ... quite the "international" slate of characters for the age. Anyway, sound like fun? It's just $3.50 in the Dover Thrift Edition (this is the last of that recent bunch that I'd ordered), so you're not likely to do better than picking that up at cover price.

Notes:

1. http://btripp-books.livejournal.com/42613.html
2-3. http://amzn.to/29MfNPt
4. http://en.wikipedia.org/wiki/Dark_Shadows
5. http://www.youtube.com/watch?v=zmcrreUVBeo
6. http://amzn.to/29MfNPt

Sunday, September 30, 2007[1]

Ah, one more for this month ...

A while back Barnes & Noble was having a clearance on their web site (and frequent readers know how I *love a sale!*) and they had these nifty little (just over 4x7") copies of The Constitution of the United States with the Declaration of Independence and the Articles of Confederation[2] for a paltry two bucks a piece. I bought *five* (giving copies to my daughters and nieces for Constitution Day a few weeks back) and keeping one for myself. Now, readers who have been paying *way* too much attention are no doubt asking "Brendan, didn't you just read this a little while back?" ... well, yes ... back in April of '06 I plowed through another edition, however, that[3] was more of a "judicial activist" review of Supreme Court meddling with this most important document, and I really wanted a basic reference in my library. This edition fits in quite nicely, with the first quarter of it being an Introduction (by law professor R.B. Bernstein) which puts the process of moving from colonies into confederated states and eventually to a Federal system with our current Constitution into its various historical, cultural, and intellectual contexts.

I'm always happy to find "new info" when reading stuff that I assume I know, and there were bits and pieces in here that I was not aware of. For instance, in the Articles of Confederation (which preceded the Constitution), under Article XI, Canada is offered a full partnership just by acceding to the terms therein (where all other colonies, etc. would require the approval of 9 states). I wonder if that offer is still "on the table"? Ah, before you scoff ... let me outline the *second* "I did not know that!" moment in this ... do you know when the most recent Constitutional Amendment was ratified? Think about it ... these things tend to be HUGE political dust-ups. The one preceding this lowered the voting age from 21 to 18 at the height of the Viet Nam angst back in 1971. Give up? The 27th Amendment was ratified in *1992*. No, I don't recall hearing anything about it either. However, I suspect this has a lot to do with it having been *proposed* in 1789 but not officially *ratified* until nearly 203 years later (it[4] has to do with paying Senators and Representatives). If a "housekeeping detail" like the 27th Amendment can be pending for two centuries, why not an open invite to our neighbors to the north to join our Republic!

Another good feature to Bernstein's introduction is a look at the sort of compromises that had to be made in drafting the Constitution ... what groups wanted what things in there, what groups didn't, why certain items (that today sound somewhat odd, like the 3rd Amendment) made it in, and why more sweeping philosophical stances didn't. It's a very enlightening read, and I do hope The Girls will eventually bother to delve into it ("eventually" as they're all between 7 and 11 at the moment, and I figure this is a "remember when" book for some time down the road).

As you can guess, I highly recommend getting a copy of this *well before* the next election (as I'm guessing that Hillary is not going to want it around!), and this is a very concise and enlightening edition. Oddly enough (or not) Amazon doesn't list this as being in print, however, BN.com as it at its (very low) $4.95 cover price. I'm guessing that it might also be in your local Barnes & Noble retailer.

Notes:

1. http://btripp-books.livejournal.com/42938.html
2. http://amzn.to/29PWMMz
3. http://btripp-books.livejournal.com/16420.html
4. https://goo.gl/a3Ocvy

Sunday, October 7, 2007[1]

Fantastic little book!

Sam Harris' Letter to a Christian Nation[2] is an *amazing* little book. As readers who have followed my reviews and journal on-going through the years know, I'm in a rather uncomfortable minority of folks who are both strongly con-servative *and* extremely anti-religion. This creates a dy-namic where I get ostracized from almost any discussion or group, as I have no tolerance on one hand for the so-cialistic fairy tales of the Left or the psychotic devotion to Imaginary Friends seen in so many on the Right. While I don't know how *conservative* Sam Harris is (I suspect not much as he gets into red-state/blue-state stuff in here, which is largely a liberal talking point), he is *totally* on-target with my views of Christianity.

Just as I have urged my readers to get books like Mona Charen's Useful Idiots[3] or Ann Coulter's Treason[4] (even those folks in the Left/Liberal camp), I would also recommend that *everybody* pick up a copy of Letter to a Chris-tian Nation[5], *especially* if you're one of those Xtian types to whom the book is addressed! Yes, this is likely to get your undies in a wad nearly as much as Coulter does for the Che t-shirt wearing crowd, but it will likewise provide perspective of *why some people think you're being delusional* (and are thereby at times rather *scary*).

Frankly, I probably stuck more little bits of paper in here for "choice passag-es" than in any book I've recently read, and I'm somewhat frustrated that I'm only going to use a few here. Harris goes into the "philosophical" aspects of morality, personal behaviors, etc. in terms of the Bible, and after offering up examples of assorted Biblical admonitions suggests:

> *Anyone who believes that the Bible offers the best guidance we have on questions of morality has some very strange ideas about either guidance or morality.*

He also discusses the Bible in the context of history and of *other* religious documents around the world (frequently wishing we had a Jain[6] "cultural heritage" rather than the rather schizophrenic Judeo-Christian one), point-ing out that:

> *If you think that Christianity is the most direct and undefiled expression of love and compassion that the world has ever seen, you do not know much about the world's other religions.*

This pretty much defines how I came to my own lack of belief ... nothing like being a Religion Major to see that the emperor is butt-naked! While I do not typically self-identify as an *atheist*, Harris has an amusing take on the term, saying that nobody has to define themselves as a "non-astrologer" or "non-alchemist", and that:

> *Atheism is nothing more than the noises reasonable people make in the presence of unjustified religious beliefs.*

... further connecting these beliefs with those such as Elvis being alive and UFOs carving up livestock.

Again, there is so much of this book that I'd enthusiastically quote here, but it's only about 100 pages long, so I'd hate to be like the trailer for a B-movie that was serving up all the "good parts" (not that Letter to a Christian Nation[7] isn't chock-full of "good parts", these are just the pithiest of the bits that jumped out at me), so I'll only add a few more here ...

> *It is time that we admitted that faith is nothing more than the license religious people give one another to keep believing when reasons fail.*
>
> *While believing strongly, without evidence, is considered a mark of madness or stupidity in any other area of our lives, faith in God still holds immense prestige in our society.*
>
> *Religion is the one area of our discourse where it is considered noble to pretend to be certain about things no human being could possibly be certain about.*

Of course, while this book is addressed to *Christians*, it is certainly applicable to *any* dogmatic religion. Early on in the text, Harris addresses Islam and how both the Koran and the Bible (among many other religious tomes) are equally insistent on their unique infallibility. If one looks at enough religions which demand belief in their being the "only truth" it eventually becomes clear that the odds that *none* are "the truth" are far higher than any *one* being true. Or, as Harris puts it:

> *Understand that the way you view Islam is precisely the way devout Muslims view Christianity. And it is the way I view all religions.*

This reminds me of the quip that "the difference between an Atheist and a Monotheist is that an Atheist disbelieves in *one more* god", putting the Monotheist's "imaginary friend" in the same dustbin that the ancient pantheons of the Christian-conquered lands were tossed.

Personally, I can't wait to be able to pass copies of this along to my kids (I tried the 11-year-old and she said that she "really didn't care about that religion and politics stuff" at the moment) when they get to a point about wondering why we don't "do church".

If I had *one* quibble with Letter to a Christian Nation[8] it would be its *pricing*. As noted above, this is only about 100 pages long, yet the hardcover is going for $16.95 ... which reminds me of Idries Shah selling what was essentially a blank book for $25 because "people don't value knowledge unless they've paid for it" ... somehow I doubt that Harris and his publisher Knopf are doing a "Sufi working" here, and this could easily have been pegged at *half* its current cover price (even the upcoming paperback edition is going to have an $11 cover). Perhaps they're counting on people like me being as enthusiastic as I am about this so that we don't care what it costs. That said, it looks like your best bet would be Amazon, which has this at 32% off, so if you combine it with other stuff to get free shipping, you'll be ahead of even the cheapest currently available new/used copy (once shipping's tacked on). Again ... this is one that I think *everybody* needs to read ... so go get a copy!

Notes:

1. http://btripp-books.livejournal.com/43169.html
2. http://amzn.to/29Fj9IA
3. http://btripp-books.livejournal.com/39941.html
4. http://btripp-books.livejournal.com/6772.html
5. http://amzn.to/29Fj9IA
6. https://en.wikipedia.org/wiki/Jainism
7-8. http://amzn.to/29Fj9IA

Saturday, October 13, 2007[1]

Hot Stuff ...

I was very excited to get this book, as it is the first I've received from any of the "review programs" out there, this coming from HarperCollins' "First Look". After putting up a hundred and sixty or so book reviews on my blog, I figured I should see what opportunities are out there, and I was happy to find Jeffrey Rothfeder's McIlhenny's Gold: How a Louisiana Family Built the Tabasco Empire[2] on their list of fall releases. As I have mentioned previously, I grew up in the P.R. end of the "consumer packaged food product" industry, and was *very* familiar with the hot sauce niche via our work with Pace Foods and others, so this should have been another of those food books which hit "close to home".

However, unless one hails from New Iberia, I'm guessing that the story spun out in McIlhenny's Gold[3] is not something which hits "close to home" for most people, because the family which brought the world Tabasco Sauce (of which I have been a great fan for a long time), is unique, insular, and extremely tied in with its very specific geographic roots. Frankly, I had *expected* this book to have been a "triumphant story" of an enterprising family arising from the ashes of the Civil War to create one of the great brand names in the world, yet (while that *is* the general story line) it's not so much a paean as an investigative report, a reality that I'm guessing arose through the McIlhenny family declining to cooperate with the author, who was then left with "official" and secondary sources, most of which are, of course, free of the "spin" the family leadership would have liked to preserve.

And, "spin" (or at least "embellished tales"), is a recurring theme here. Indeed, in my mind, the ghost of Justin Wilson (a Cajun "raconteur" and TV Chef best remembered for deep-frying a Thanksgiving turkey) hovered as a recognizable figure of the sort of person that most of the McIlhenny's appeared to be ... which helped, as the book is bereft of pictures, leading to having to imagine much of the people and places (I'd recommend a visit to the Tabasco web site[4] to fill in a few of the blanks) ... with instance after instance of the "family line" not exactly being what an outsider (be they at the patent office or a competitor's boardroom) would consider "the truth".

The story opens in the antebellum south, with D.D. Avery marrying into the Marsh family, and eventually taking over ownership of Isle Petit Anse, the bayou island that would subsequently bear his name, and the sugar plantations run on it. The pivotal player in the family myth, Edmund McIlhenny (son of a Scottish tavern-owner in Maryland) had made a fortune in the evolving banking industry, and (after years of business relations with the family) ended up marrying one of Avery's daughters. The families fled the area during the Civil War, only to return to devastation, with the New Orleans banking industry wiped out, and Avery Island ravaged (the Union had captured the island for its extensive salt deposits). The "official story" was that Edmund had gotten some "exotic" Mexican pepper seeds and sowed them in a garden plot, resulting in the initial peppers used for Tabasco sauce, however, another Louisiana businessman (with connections to both McIlhenny and the Averys) had been producing a Tabasco pepper-based sauce well before the war, and it appears that the "official story" is a myth to cover up the likelihood that producing a pepper sauce was "plan C" for a family trying to get back on its feet.

Of course, the pepper sauce that Edmund McIlhenny began producing on Avery Island was quite a success and the "iffy" truth of its origins should not diminish the fact that taking this route made the McIlhenny family one of the great names of Louisiana, and a world-wide recognizable brand. Over time, McIlhenny, as Avery had before him, consolidated his ownership of the island, creating a business that was solidly linked to his family line ... a reality which would "flavor" the business for most of its history, and perhaps doom it in the end. In many ways, McIlhenny's Gold[5] is a "serial biography", as it moves down the generations, from Edmund to John Avery McIlhenny (a Rough-Rider and long-time associate of Teddy Roosevelt), to Edward Avery McIlhenny (a noted naturalist and traveler, who ended giving Avery island some of its most unique features), to Walter Stauffer McIlhenny (a renowned WW2 hero known as "Tabasco Mac") who died in 1985. Each of these men had a particular style, and related to the family, company, and island in different ways, but each having a devotion to the product.

Unfortunately, the story becomes muddled with Walter's death. While there never had been a clear "line of succession" for the top job at the company, somebody was always there to step up and make his mark. Somehow, at the 5th generation, there was no clear choice. Also, due to the stipulation that all company stock must stay within the family (and there being between one and two hundred descendants making some sort of a living off of the company's profits), there were serious "boardroom battles" between factions. Eventually, Edward Simmons (grandson of Edward McIlhenny) was pushed into the big chair. The following years were tumultuous, and Simmon's tenure was ended when Paul McIlhenny managed to obtain enough stock to force a change to his (current) leadership.

As noted, I have been a great fan of Tabasco Sauce, and I would have hoped that McIlhenny's Gold[6] was a "happier" story. While fascinating reading, one feels worry for the continuation of the product, at least as the iconic presence that it has been all my life. Certainly anybody with an interest in food in general, and in hot sauces in particular, should read this book, as should those wishing to peer through a window into the very strange world of the deepest south, and how the Civil War changed the lives of the leaders of that society. I see from both Amazon and B&N that this book is already available (at 34% and 20% discounts respectively), so I assume you can likewise find it at your local brick-and-mortar book vendor.

Notes:

1. http://btripp-books.livejournal.com/43365.html

2-3. http://amzn.to/2abmUiH

4. http://tabasco.com/tabasco_history/index.cfm

5-6. http://amzn.to/2abmUiH

Sunday, October 14, 2007[1]

Important stuff ...

I usually try to keep my reviews coming in the same order as I've read the books (the same way that I keep things cataloged over on LibraryThing[2]), but every now and again I find myself with a stack of things I've just finished reading (a hazard of having 2-3 books going at any one time), and one just begs to get reviewed first. That was the case this weekend, and I really felt I should knock out the review of that Tabasco book first while the specifics were still fresh in my mind.

This is not to say that I've been letting Common Sense, The Rights of Man and Other Essential Writings of Thomas Paine[3] "go stale" in my head, but the two books are very different, and much of what I'm going to say about this is based on quotations, and not "impressions", so it was the easier one to put aside for a couple of days.

I have, of late, been filling in lacunae in my general education, bits and pieces that I'm running across *now*, that, on reflection, I probably should have read in highschool or college ... and Thomas Paine is certainly in that category. Of course, I was familiar enough with Paine, the titles of his works and their general drift, that I wouldn't *embarrass* myself in a discussion which referred to them, but I realized that I had very likely not read these except in various excerpts during my school career. The present volume presents his *Common Sense* and both volumes of *Rights of Man* in their entirety and includes "selections from" *The Crisis*, *The Age Of Reason*, and *Agrarian Justice*.

Frankly, my interest in catching up on Paine (and other revolutionary writers from the Enlightenment) dates back to some reading I did earlier this year, such as Brooke Allen's excellent Moral Minority[4] ... further being fascinated by running into random quotes such as Teddy Roosevelt's slamming Paine as a *"filthy little atheist"*. Needless to say, I was surprised (OK, *disappointed*) by the "conventional Christian" setting of most everything in this book. Obviously, I need to track down a complete volume of *The Age of Reason* where Paine *does* let go with some delicious broadsides, and provides "rational context" on how so many otherwise sensible people can be delusional about their imaginary friends, an analysis as to the point today as it was two centuries back:

> *That many good men have believed this strange fable, and lived very good lives under that belief (for credulity is not a crime) is what I have no doubt of. In the first place, they were educated to believe it, and they would have believed any thing else in the same manner. There are also many who have been so enthusiastically enraptured by what they conceived to be the infinite love of God to man, in making a sacrifice of himself, that the vehemence of the idea has forbidden and deterred them from*

> *examining into the absurdity and profaneness of the story. The more unnatural any thing is, the more it is capable of becoming the object of dismal admiration.*

... interestingly, Paine only penned *The Age Of Reason* when he was expecting to be soon dead, saying *"I intended it to be the last offering I should make to my fellow citizens of all nations"*, however he lived on another 15 years after its release, no doubt regretting the timing! Again, there are only 20 pages of this classic in here (and most editions I've looked at on-line are over 150 pages), so this is something that I will have to put on my "to read" list.

The main parts of this book reflect Paine's literary support of the American and French revolutions. *Common Sense* being an anonymously-written pamphlet (which thereby netted him zero for the royalties of as many as half a million copies printed during the course of the Revolution!), with various follow-ups all released in the first two months of 1776. It is easy to see how Paine is much beloved of modern Libertarians in lines like:

> *"Society is produced by our wants, and government by wickedness; the former promotes our happiness positively by uniting our affections, the latter negatively by restraining our vices. The one encourages intercourse, the other creates distinctions. The first is a patron, the last a punisher. Society in every state is a blessing, but government even in its best state is but a necessary evil."*

Over half this volume consists of *The Rights of Man* which is Paine's defense of the French Revolution against the attacks of Edmund Burke, an Irish statesman who had supported the American Revolution, but strongly opposed the revolution in France. Paine goes beyond countering Burke (a former friend), and spins out a treatise on natural rights, although, to this modern reader, the details of the French court are hazy ghosts which make the reading somewhat anachronistic. Here too are found threads of the sort of clear-headedness which inspired *The Age of Reason*:

> *"With respect to what are called denominations of religion, if every one is left to judge of his own religion, there is no such thing as a religion that is wrong; but if they are to judge of each other's religion, there is no such thing as a religion that is right; and therefore all the world is right, or all the world is wrong."*

Needless to say, it is a shame that Thomas Paine's words are not better known in these dark days of our Republic! It is not enough to advocate a return to the *political* vision of men the likes of Washington and Jefferson, we really must seek a return to the type of Deism, a personal, non-aggressive faith, that these men likewise espoused, and saw as a keystone to the success of a nation such as ours.

I would certainly recommend picking up a copy of <u>Common Sense, The Rights of Man and Other Essential Writings of Thomas Paine</u>[5] if you'd like to get "caught up" on some of the theoretical underpinnings of the American political experiment. This volume is a Signet Classic, and is priced very reasonably at $5.95 ... so you might as well go looking for it at your local brick-and-mortar store, or add it on to an internet order some time when you're looking for "something extra" to push the total into the free shipping zone.

Notes:

1. http://btripp-books.livejournal.com/43679.html
2. http://btripp-books.com/
3. http://amzn.to/29G5Z9g
4. http://btripp-books.livejournal.com/33522.html
5. http://amzn.to/29G5Z9g

Wednesday, October 17, 2007[1]

Oh, what fun ...

You know, a lot of the time I'll read one of Ann's books and charge off saying that "everybody should read this!" (even those Che t-shirt wearing dreamers who peruse my scribblings here) because she's Speaking The Truth and is making points that Everybody Needs To Hear. Well, not this time. The latest salvo from Ann Coulter, If Democrats Had Any Brains, They'd Be Republicans[2] is strictly a "guilty pleasure" for those of us who are Ann fans.

Now, I must admit, I "took a pass" on her previous book, *Godless*, because it was based on her inexplicable infatuation with her Imaginary Friend and the socially ingrained organizations which exist to prop up that delusion. If only Ann were *deeply agnostic* on the religion front, she'd be the shining light of sarcasm for the age, but I guess every hero needs clay feet in some form, and her religious credulity (with its associated spin-offs into being seriously wrong about a whole lot of science) appears to be her "Achilles' heel". I figured that if Ann was insisting on embarrassing herself (yeah, like *that's* possible), I should at least look away when the feathers hit the floor.

Anyhow, unlike brilliant surveys like *Slander* and *Treason* (which I **do** recommend that everybody read), where Ann is out to Prove A Point, this is another collection of bits and pieces (culled from her books, columns, speeches, interviews, and TV appearances), specifically chosen to poke sharp sticks at the Left (quote: *"I think liberals have missed some of my zestier quotes, which is why we've decided to compile this volume"*). Needless to say, I found the book *hilarious* and a delightful read (minus the occasional anti-Darwin blithering), but I would hardly expect that anybody to the left of Dennis Miller would find anything funny about this (well, perhaps with the exception of noting that her most frequent quote is *"May I please finish my thought, Alan?"*, directed, of course, to the simpering weasel that Sean Hannity has to put up with day in and day out).

So, yes, I did stick my little bits of paper in the book as I breezed through this, and so have a few choice goodies to pass along to you!

> "Clinton's defense was essentially that he is not impeachable because his conduct is so disreputable that the framers could not have conceived of it."

> "Today's college liberals ape the beliefs of 99 percent of their professors and then pretend they're on -the-edge radicals."

> "Liberals titter about conservatives imagining Communists under every bed, while they hysterically claim to see racists under every bed. If, in addition to murdering tens of millions of people, Stalin had

> maintained "Whites only" water fountains, America would now celebrate a national Joe McCarthy Day."
>
> "If the death penalty doesn't deter murder, how come Michael Moore is still alive and I'm not on death row?"
>
> "Liberals are either traitors or idiots, and on the matter of America's self-preservation, the difference is irrelevant."

And, in a closing quip functioning somewhat as an Afterword, she adds:

> "Finally, a word to those of you out there who have yet to be offended by something I have written or said: Please be patient. I am working as fast as I can."

Needless to say, if this small sampling sounds like good fun to you, go pick up a copy of If Democrats Had Any Brains, They'd Be Republicans[3]! Being that this is new, it should be in all the brick-and-mortar bookmongers in your area (although no doubt hidden on the shelves by self-righteous quasi-Marxist store staff), however I got my copy via Amazon at their current discount price, which is a whopping 40% off of cover. I'm sure that if you wait a year or so this will be cheap via the new/used vendors, but right now you'll be paying more (with shipping) via them than getting Amazon's discount price and adding a couple of things up to the free shipping zone.

Notes:

1. http://btripp-books.livejournal.com/43927.html

2-3. http://amzn.to/29KGZhw

Sunday, October 21, 2007[1]

An odd one ...

As I've noted from time-to-time in these little reviews, there was a point (back when I was a P.R. executive) when I had a lot of money and would buy a lot of books, often sight unseen from various catalogs. As I've also related, I have quite a few boxes (used to be bookshelves, but I've been rotating out the unread books as I get new stuff finished) of "to be read" books stacked up around here, and every now and again I end up looking at my "active" to-be-read piles and am uninspired by the current queue and go digging into those boxes. Well, for *some reason* From Clocks to Chaos: The Rhythms of Life[2] by Leon Glass and Michael C. Mackey (professors of physiology at McGill University) grabbed my attention and I slogged into it.

Now, I don't recall *getting* this book, and I assume that it came in with a bunch of other math/science books, being sort of about "Chaos", and this would have been a fairly likely purchase for me in the late '80s to early '90s. Frankly, it's a bit of an odd book ... it takes a look at biological systems from a mathematical standpoint, or roughly the title of chapter 2: *"Steady States, Oscillations, and Chaos in Physiological Systems"*. The authors note that most researchers in the biological sciences are not particularly mathematically inclined (or trained) and point out that these systems, were they exhibiting these patterns in any other context, would be likely to have been long since subjected to *"mathematical models subsumed under the rubric 'Theory of Dynamical Systems'"*. The authors attempt to fill this gap by *"the applications of mathematics to the study of normal and pathological physiological rhythms"*.

One other thing to note about this book, it is pretty clearly intended as a textbook, and its target would seem to be upper-level undergraduates, and while they make a valiant effort to "buffer" the mathematics involved (shunting much of it off to a rather extensive, and somewhat hard-to-follow, appendix), there still is quite a lot of complex equations being thrown around, along with various charts and graphs to illustrate what's going on in the math. Oh, and if the sub-title "The Rhythms of Life" gets you humming tunes from *The Lion King*, this is a book that would get P.E.T.A. fuming as almost every "rhythm" measured involves probes stuck into cats, dogs, rats, etc., some alive (but paralyzed), some "in vitro". Even I got creeped out about this, and "animal rights" stuff almost never registers with me (one footnote did report on the possibility of a particular researcher dying from doing an experimental study on his own heart ... so there are *some* researchers who aren't cutting open Rover to see what makes him tick).

Well, at this point, I'm guessing 90-95% of folks looking at these pixels have already decided that they're not likely to want to check out From Clocks to Chaos[3], but not only is it obscure, difficult, and somewhat squicky ... it also has blocks of prose like this to contend with:

> The locus of all points with the same latent phase is called an **isochron**. An isochron is a smooth curve (for limit cycles in two dimensions) crossing the trajectories in the attractor basin of the limit cycle. The state point on any trajectory in the attractor basin of the limit cycle passes through all the isochrons at uniform rate. Thus isochrons are very close together whenever time derivatives are small. In particular, isochrons come arbitrarily close together at any fixed point and therefore necessarily also along any singular trajectory leading to a fixed point. The locus of stationary states and attracting sets of these stationary states is called the **phaseless set**. Except for the phaseless set, one and only one isochron passes through each point in the attractor basin of the limit cycle.

Aside from loving the phrase "attractor basin" (which is quite evocative for some chaos models), who's going to *get* something like that on the first read-through? It certainly doesn't help that the next paragraph launches into an equation with *cos 2πφ'* on the left side of the equals sign (never mind what's on the right, but it's not pretty) ... and much of the book goes like this!

Anyway, the other clue that this is a textbook is that it's still in print 20 years later, and that the cover price is a whopping $45.00 ... sure it has over 30 pages of references, but that's *steep*. If for some inexplicable reason all the above has whetted your appetite for just this sort of mental snack, it *is* available via the new/used vendors for as little as $4.27 (before shipping) for a "very good" copy. However, needless to say, this is one that we can chalk up to "Brendan needed a particular brain input" and not feel deprived that you haven't read it too!

Notes:

1. http://btripp-books.livejournal.com/44108.html

2-3. http://amzn.to/29DGXo6

Sunday, October 28, 2007[1]

Seven and Mountains and Bears ... OH MY!

Having not quite un-tired of the topics in my current "to be read" piles of books, I went diving into my various file boxes of older stuff that got rotated off the "to be read" *shelves* as those spaces were needed for recent completed reads (and, yes, that dreaded "out of shelf space" zone *is* hovering on the horizon now). Like the math book[2] which preceded it here, this had been likely waiting for me to get to it for the better part of two decades.

Naturally, one of the problems with picking up an older book, especially one "groping its way through" a murky or complex subject, is that one is never *quite* sure where the information falls in terms of "present knowledge". Now, as noted in previous reviews, when dealing with some cutting-edge physics, it's reasonably easy to triangulate what's "preliminary" and what's just "early", but in stuff like Geoffrey Ashe's Dawn Behind the Dawn: A Search for the Earthly Paradise[3] it's hard to gauge. Ashe, a "cultural historian" specializing in sorting through myths to find their historical roots (most notably in the Arthurian material), had previously published a book on "ancient wisdom" and had been badgered by the response to that to looking into some of the theories of the likes of Marija Gimbutas, of there having been some "golden age" of a matriarchal peaceful culture that was crushed beneath the wheels of the Aryan expansion.

I was worried early on, as, while Gimbutas is a respected researcher, Ashe floated into using Starhawk as a "source" ... fortunately, this appears to have only been to set a mark as to the extents that the "Goddess stuff" can go, and did not base much, if any, of the rest of the book on that material. In fact, Ashe seems careful to "skate around" many "non-academics" (he does briefly discuss Blavatsky, but never mentions Sitchin, although he could well "have gone there" in context), and keep his discussions to "standard research" sources.

Unfortunately, the book ends up looking at a LOT of cultures over a large expanse of both territory and time, so it makes doing a "thumbnail sketch" of it difficult. Ultimately, it considers the possibility that there was a "northern homeland" (he calls it a cultural "seedbed") which is recalled in the myths of the Hyperboreans, Shambhala, Mount Meru, etc., and how one might be able to find traces of that in surviving cultural and archaeological remnants. There are several elements which he follows, but these eventually boil down to a core three, the number 7 as an "organizing grid" (think the days of the week), the idea of a "holy mountain" (be it Meru, Zion, or even Purgatory), and "the Bear" in various contexts. Much of the latter arises from Shamanic practices (and he argues that the Shamanism found in the Americas is a linear survival of that practiced in Asia when there still was a land bridge), with a fascinating factoid that in all the early cultural traces, each north Asian tribal group had a very similar name for a *female* shaman (something like *"utygan"*), but had widely varying names for *male* shamans ... indicating that the practice was initially a women's rite, only later co-opted by the men. Also, in some of these languages, the same word meant "bear". The significance of the number 7, he believes, is ultimately based on the stars of the Great Bear, which in antiquity circled the pole when there was no well-defined pole star. The other element that seems to have moved with these is "proto-Artemis", a Goddess (who with her brother Apollo) seems to crop up in various forms in numerous places. One side note that I was amazed that he "didn't pull the trigger on" was pointing out that *Arthur* is a "bear name" (despite his noting that "arth-" is a prefix indicating "bear" in Welsh and related tongues) ... I guess Ashe felt that pulling in his Arthurian work was only going to confuse matters more!

Anyway, he traces these threads through India (and the *Rig-Veda*), Tibet (and the *Kalachakra* materials), the Caspian, Mesopotamia, Greece, and Israel. His thesis eventually becomes that the early Indo-Europeans, rather than being the "conquerors" of the early Goddess culture, had branches which settled very early in north-central Asia (the Altai range of mountains, whose Mount Belukha {pictured here[4]} would be the "cultural memory" model of all the subsequent "sacred mountains"), and *then* began their expansions into India, Iran, and Europe, carrying with them the "Bear/7" model and the "Artemis" Goddess lore (which would re-surface in various settings, when given the chance). One of the most fascinating "hints" dropped in here is that post-Babylon Jewish practice was deeply stamped with this model, from the 7-pillared Menorah (and the multitude of 7s in the Bible) to the possibility that "temple period" JHVH was something of a admixture of an early tribal sky-god with the Apollo aspects of the Artemis/Apollo duad ... thus leading to both Christianity (which formalized the 7 pattern for most of the world), and Islam being simply degenerate Apollonian cults which had lost all sense of their true roots!

As you can tell by my flailing around in the above, Ashe covers a LOT of stuff in this book, and backs it up with over six hundred foot-noted references and nearly two hundred cited works. While being something of a muddle (maybe it's me, but this book seemed to "reel like a drunk" in getting from point A to its eventual conclusion), it's certainly a substantially *researched* muddle! This is one of those books that's a bit hard to follow, but is so filled with little "I did *not* know that!" gems that it's quite endearing. I don't know if I've attained any new wisdom from having read this, but I'm glad I went through the journey.

Dawn Behind the Dawn[5] is out of print in both hardcover and paperback at this point, but is available through the used vendors with "very good" hardcover copies for under a buck and new copies of the paperback for around three bucks (plus shipping, of course). If you have any interest in "this sort of stuff", it would certainly be a good addition to your library!

Notes

1. http://btripp-books.livejournal.com/44297.html
2. http://btripp-books.livejournal.com/44108.html
3. http://amzn.to/29Fh611
4. https://goo.gl/QcfQ4L
5. http://amzn.to/29Fh611

Sunday, November 4, 2007[1]

An excellent Shamanic book ...

As I've noted here previously, I studied with Alberto Villoldo for an extended period, from the early 80's through the mid-90's and was on hand for a number of the events covered in his early books. Unfortunately, this familiarity created a certain dissonance for me in many of those books, as they were *highly* "fictionalized" and rarely tracked with actual time-lines (I later found that this was substantially an artifact of Alberto's early approach to his books, dropping off a couple of file boxes full of notepads, journals, and assorted scraps of paper to Eric Jendresen who'd then attempt to make a coherent story of them).

However, Alberto's recent books do appear to be his own expressions, and his most recent, The Four Insights: Wisdom, Power, and Grace of the Earthkeepers[2], is an excellent example of his teaching approach. Frankly, when I finished reading this, I felt like I had just gone through a weekend workshop with Alberto, and that is perhaps the best way to approach his new books.

Again, I have certain difficulties "filtering" via a lens of previous contexts and data when approaching this material. Alberto has "re-framed" much material from several South American shamanic traditions into one "mythologized" group of "the Laika" whose particulars sound to be congruent with the high-mountain Q'ero tribes. As I was *not* around for the past decade or so, I don't know how this assimilation evolved (the last few times I did stuff with Alberto he was just getting involved with the Q'ero), but it does serve to provide a unified "voice" for the teachings rather than tagging this bit as being from some Amazonian group, that bit from some Quechuan tradition, etc.

The Four Insights[3] is largely based on a "medicine wheel" format, of the Serpent, the Jaguar, the "Hummingbird" (in many other traditions, something like a Buffalo or Horse), and the Eagle, linked to organic, intellectual/emotional, soul, and spirit awarenesses, and in turn to "The Way of the Hero", "The Way of the Luminous Warrior", "The Way of the Seer", and "The Way of the Sage". Alberto spends the first fifth of the book "setting the stage" for these, and then walking the reader through each of the "ways", with specific orientations and exercises for each. As I said, reading through this was very much like progressing through a workshop on the material (but without having to take notes!).

I found some *fascinating* bits and pieces in The Four Insights[4], including Alberto's briefly touching on "the assemblage point" (more familiar from the Castaneda books). It appears that Alberto has spent some time working with this concept (which I don't recall him using before), both intellectually and energetically, and presents some direct instructions and exercises involving it (elements certainly absent from Castaneda). I had a big "AHA!" moment when I read this:

> In the West, the assemblage point tends to be located to one side of the head because we're very rational, thought-driven people. We're attracted to others who have an assemblage point that is similar in valance and position because we feel in sync with them. We typically perceive someone with a very difference assemblage point as strange or foolish, and we may even think that they're stupid because they can't perceive what we can, or loony because they sense what we don't.

Now, as readers of my journal know, I "have issues" with both religion and liberalism, and frequently am frustrated when I find otherwise intelligent people who believe in "imaginary friends" or clearly "delusional politics". The model of *"out of sync assemblage points"* could go a long way towards explaining why some people, despite being smart, decent human beings, could be so *wrong* about key existential subjects!

Another thing that Alberto introduces here is a concept of a "bridge" position for the assemblage point, which is where it would be *""if we lived in perfect communion with nature"*, but is, functionally, a center position through which movements of the assemblage point must shift. His descriptions of the "experiential state" of this "bridge" zone greatly resembled what Eckhart Tolle described as the "Now" perception, and gives this a functionality that's not really in Tolle's book.

One "tidbit" that Alberto injects in his discussion of "The Luminous Warrior" is a brain-structure element that I had not seen described elsewhere (and I sure wish there had been footnotes so I could have checked the sources on this):

> *Our propensity toward violent solutions is rooted in our brains, which are wired in a very strange way. The region where our sensations of pleasure are experienced is very close to the center where we experience violence, so when we stimulate one of these areas in the brain, we often end up stimulating the other*

He then goes on to note that Humans are the only mammal "wired" this way. This could go a long way to understanding the success of our species up to this point (let alone almost defining the appeal of *Valhalla*), but also as a warning about how we're likely to react in any given modern situation.

Obviously, The Four Insights[5] operates on may different levels. Alberto has gotten to a point where he seems effortlessly able to weave through mythic, symbolic, literal, and academic threads in his exposition of the "Laika" teachings. An example of this which jumped out at me was in his description of how the high shamanic practitioners would approach a problem in "The Way of the Seer" section:

> *Indigenous alchemy is made up of four steps: identification, differentiation, integration, and transcendence. Identification is the quality of serpent; differ-*

> *entiation, of jaguar; integration, of hummingbird; and transcendence, of eagle.*

This, in a discussion which also references Claude Lévi-Strauss and Ken Wilbur. All through the book, Villoldo "anchors" his information in real-world examples (of his students and clients), puts the material "in context" of the current literature of the study of consciousness (and that of cutting-edge physical and medical sciences), bolsters the "theory" with exercises that pretty much anybody can master, yet stays true to the feeling that this is "passing on ancient wisdom" from Shamanic teachers.

Needless to say, I highly recommend this book. Despite its "newagey" title (and I assume that much of these trappings come from Hay House's marketing arm), this is a very cogent, balanced, and rational look at the Shamanic world-view which would be beneficial for anybody to read. It's also very reasonably priced at only $12.95 cover for the paperback, so you'd not break the bank picking it up at your local brick-and-mortar store ... Amazon, however has it at 20% off, which works out better (assuming combining it with other stuff to get free shipping) than any of the current new/used vendor deals. Even if you've not read any of Villoldo's previous books, do check this one out!

Notes:

1. http://btripp-books.livejournal.com/44577.html

2-5. http://amzn.to/29FnRRu

Friday, November 9, 2007[1]

Another book that EVERYBODY should read ...

Due to time issues with my new job, I've gotten behind on my review-writing, and that's meant this current book has "cooled" a bit while waiting a week for me to get around to dealing with it. Frankly, when I was half-way through reading this, I was thinking that Sam Harris' The End of Faith: Religion, Terror, and the Future of Reason[2] was the best book *ever* and I was trying to track down bulk orders for it so that I could give copies to everybody I know! With some distance, I still feel that this is a *very important* book, and one that should be read by all and sundry, but with a few more caveats than when I was only half-way through with it.

As one might suspect, part of the reason for this is that the first half of The End of Faith[3] is far stronger than the second half. The first four chapters, *Reason in Exile*, *The Nature of Belief*, *In the Shadow of God*, and *The Problem with Islam*, present as stark and compelling argument for atheism as any I've read, dealing with the decline in rational thought since the heights of The Enlightenment, what's wrong with religion in general, the horrors that religion has wrought on humanity, and the particular perversion which is Islam (the six solid pages of "fatwa-justifying" quotes from the Koran is chilling enough). As much as I'd like to pad out this review with arch quotes from the text, I had to give up on that idea after only a few pages, as sentence after sentence *screamed* to be quoted, and it was obvious that I was not going to be able to bookmark "highlights" ... it's just *that* amazing.

However, Harris, while not weakening his polemics, changes directions in the second half. While the first half stands as a "statement for the ages", much of the second has, even now, a feeling of being "soon to be dated", especially the chapter *West of Eden* where he addresses how religion (and, obviously, fundamentalist Christianity) is corrupting Western, and especially American, society and government. From here the book turns into more of a "morality/psychology" survey, first with *A Science of Good and Evil*, and then *"Experiments in Consciousness"*, which is (as one would guess) a look at possible ways of transcending religion.

Personally, I wish he'd done *two* books ... rounding out the first half with a chapter or two of more "rallying the troops" (and he is, with me, certainly "preaching to the choir" there), and then presenting a more "newagey" look at "what's wrong with religion, and what to do about it" as a second title.

To be honest, Harris significantly undercuts himself in that last chapter, as he reveals that he is a meditator and a quasi-Buddhist practitioner. Now, while Buddhism is, by definition a "non-theistic" creed, it is certainly framed, both within and without, *as a religion*, so advocating practices and approaches associated with that creates a certain dissonance in his allies, and provides a huge "stick" with which his enemies can attack the rest of his thesis. I mean, it is *one thing* to hold out Jainism (as other atheists frequently do) as a "harmless" and/or relatively "sensible" religion, and *another* to be advocating "the wisdom of the east" as a solution to the problem of religion.

While his *point* in this is quite well taken (that Western philosophy and the accompanying monotheisms have produced less truly introspective material than Islam has quotes supporting it being "the religion of peace"), it does read like *"a confusing eruption of speculative philosophy"* in context.

Had Harris done two books, I would be standing on the street corner handing out copies of the first, which is not to say that the second is weak or wrong or not extremely worthwhile; but I do feel it's unfortunate that this plays out the way it does. Certainly, religious fundamentalists will use the latter material as a straw man to attack the earlier, a situation for which Harris "leaves the door open". Of course, I also feel bad about bringing this up as a criticism, as nearly *everything* that he brings up in that final chapter I (who have also studied Buddhism and various other Eastern systems) heartily agree with.

All that being said, I *highly* recommend getting a copy of The End of Faith[4]! It's in print (so will be at the local bookstore), is very reasonably priced at $13.95 (Amazon has it at 20% off), and really deserves to be part of the culture's basic discussion.

Notes:

1. http://btripp-books.livejournal.com/44948.html
2-4. http://amzn.to/29CY2hP

Saturday, November 10, 2007[1]

An "interesting" book ...

Every now and again, I get into a book that makes me have to look at some of my biases, and this was one of them. While John McCrone's The Ape That Spoke: Language and the Evolution of the Human Mind[2] was *interesting*, I kept wondering how *real* it was, and this was in no small part due to my not being able to dig up anything about the author.

Despite Googling quite a bit, "John McCrone" seems to have very few traces; he appears to be a journalist of some sort, yet was noted in one place as being something of a "crank". This, coupled with his odd endnotes (they flow along generally with the text, by page number, giving a sense of where he picked up bits of info, but not actually *referencing* much) and the fact that way too many of them indicate *"mostly my own speculation"* (which is dandy if you're an "expert" in a particular field, but I could pull the same quality of speculations out of "my hat" which doesn't mean they're worth building a book on), made me wonder while reading this just how worthwhile this was.

This is not to say that what McCrone has postulated in The Ape That Spoke[3] isn't *plausible*, it's just not terribly well supported. He does go back to some very basic forms of life, sea slugs, for example, to show how "learning" can happen in even reasonably uncomplicated neural system, and projects this into the various predecessors of man, and his model of "nets" has a ring to truth to it, it's just that the *feel* of the book is like that of "armchair cosmologists" who posit theories divorced from the rigors of mathematics or the applicable physics.

The book, generally speaking, moves from early hominids, noting comparative brain size to other apes, and through the various developmental stages leading up to humanity. There were a few physiological bits in here that I'd not heard of before (such as the voice box not "dropping" in the throat in children until about age 1, allowing them to swallow and breathe at the same time for nursing, or how the human oral cavity is particularly arched, compared to our close relatives, allowing for more complicated speech, etc.), which would have been more persuasive had the referencing been more traditional. One of the fascinating concepts is that "inner speech" provided a "time delay" mechanism that allowed the developing human mind to become self-reflective, constantly watching (and labeling) what had just happened in the flow of processed experiences.

Interestingly, McCrone seems to hold that consciousness is solely a "pro cess" of the biological equipment, and the times of mental quietude (the "Now" of Tolle or samadhi experience of Zen and other disciplines) is simply returning to an animal-like blankness and that there is nothing there *but* the constant mental chatter.

> "... our sense of being conscious is an active process rather than some phantom object. Consciousness is the label for what we experience when the brain repeatedly matches incoming nets and memory to put together a string of understanding. As soon as the brain stops working - or even drops below a certain threshold of activity - consciousness evaporates. Consciousness is not something inside our heads that does all our experiencing of life for us. It is simply the description of the stream of recognition flashes that take place as long as our brains are at work ..."

As fatalistic as *that* sounds (and, admittedly, it echoes some concepts of the fascinating Zen Physics[4] book I've referenced previously), McCrone does suggest that the human brain is *malleable* enough (he gives examples of how various areas of the brain have developed *very* recently to process speech, etc.) to be adapting to new technological realities, giving examples that were quite prophetic in 1991 (which was, after all, the year that the Web was first launched, and the cutting edge chip was the 486!).

Again, there is a lot to think about in this book, but, due to the caveats noted, there was the feeling hanging over it that one *might* just be following the blitherings of some guy a couple of stools down the bar, rather than a sober discussion of the possibilities suggested by current knowledge. However, if this sparks your interest, it does appear to be out of print but you can get a "very good" used copy of the hardcover (I have a paperback version which I suspect was a bookclub imprint of the fist US edition) for *a penny* (an even $4 with shipping), so there's no major reason *not* to pick up a copy if it sounds like something you'd like to check out.

Notes:

1. http://btripp-books.livejournal.com/45166.html
2-3. http://amzn.to/29FiLFe
4. http://btripp-books.livejournal.com/7525.html

Friday, November 16, 2007[1]

"... to the uninitiated marvelous gibberish ..."

I am allowing the possibility that much of Ernest G. McClain's Myth of Invariance: The Origins of the Gods, Mathematics and Music from the Rg Veda to Plato[2] might be comprehensible for somebody with a background in musical theory, but to me it was less-than marvelous gibberish.

I have to admit that, despite many attempts over my 50 years, I have never been able to "get" music and it has always seemed an incomprehensible jumble of unnecessary complexity (why isn't a sound a certain discrete number of cycles per second, reproducible via electronics? what the hell does it *mean* to be flinging around ratios like 531441:524288?) to describe something that I can *hum* ... heck, I had to go look up even as basic stuff as which little doo-dad meant "sharp" and which meant "flat" (I will credit the author with at least cogently explaining to me what something *being* sharp or flat actually meant, a factoid that had previously not managed to sink in).

I have had *dozens* of people try to explain key, notes, etc. to me, and (aside from the basic "timing" elements, i.e. that a particular form of note represents a sound held for a particular duration) it has *never* made a lick of sense to me. As such, I'm probably not the ideal person to offer up opinions on a book which is deeply enmeshed in music theory. However, I know a lot about Gods, Indian classics, and am at least conversant in a wide array of ancient cultures, so I figured I'd finally give this one (which has been sitting around on shelves and in boxes for over 20 years) a go.

This starts plausibly enough, as the Rg Veda has been preserved as a *sung* piece, and so there could well be some musical theory enmeshed in the (admittedly odd) text. And the early bits of building a "tone mandala" from various pebbles or whatever seemed reasonable enough in the context of ancient India. And I'm assuming that some of the circular "mandala" charting, etc., is standard in music theory, but, really ... this is even hard to talk about given that HTML doesn't really even have "sharp" and "flat" characters ... *what* does one make of:

> To appreciate the necessity for "sacrifice" and the elegance of the Kalpa and Brahma yantras it will help to examine the various approximations to Ab = G# = $\sqrt{2}$ = 1.414$^+$. We have never used 7/5 = 1.4 which looks so very convenient; its reciprocal would require our "cosmological numbers" to be multiplied by 7, and to no advantage, for the ratio 45/32 (= 740/512) = 1.40625 is closer to $\sqrt{2}$ and has been with us since Chart 8. Our new "Brahmin" G# computed directly from the reference D, our "linch-pin", gives the ratio 729/512 (i.e., 3^6 divided by the nearest power of 2) = 1.423, a slightly worse

> value, and its reciprocal will require a still larger yantra to be put to sleep in integer form.

Interestingly (or, perhaps, *frustratingly*), the author was going to end the book once he'd gotten done trying to attribute each and every numerical mention of anything in the Rg Veda to some obscure musical datum. However, in discussing the book with an associate, the suggestion that YHVH of the Hebrews was simply an echo of this Indian "system" arose, and so he launched off after *other* cultures, first looking at calendrical systems (which "of course" were based on music theory ... huh?), the Book of Revelations (which is, admittedly, as incoherent as the Rg Veda with blithering numerology), backtracks to Babylon and Sumer, returns to Mt. Meru (which he suggests is simply one of his "yantras"), then plows into Plato with a re-framing of the Atlantis myth as simply some complicated "yantras" or "mandalas" conveniently convoluted to fit the numbers, and finally ending up in the Egyptian Book of the Dead, where he posits this whopper:

> The seventy-two conspirators who helped Typhon dismember Osiris must have known that 72 is the *least common denominator* by which the Osiris pentatonic scale can be expressed in integers *which remain invariant under reciprocation*

Yeah ... somehow the line *"sorry, Apu, you can't come along, that would make 73 of us, and that would screw up the math!"* just never made it onto the temple wall.

Frankly, reading this was like taking a long car trip with an old (and mathematically-obsessed) friend of mine who would see four Chevys and a stray dog and be convinced it was a SIGN from the Universe about some insane thing or another. Heck, most of this book reminds me of a story about UFO fanatics who, when finally convinced that the cloud they photographed was not, in fact, a UFO, claimed that the sneaky aliens were hiding *behind* the cloud. Again, this may be because I just don't "get" Music, but the numbers in here seem to be totally arbitrary, it doesn't seem to *matter* what exponent of 2, 3, or 5 is taken as long as it can be tortuously warped back around to some pre-determined ratio! I guess it's a good thing that (seemingly) in this "music math" any number can be twisted around to equal anything one wants.

Needless to say, I can't recommend this one to *anybody*. If you are mathematically or musically inclined, I'm guessing that there are as many glaring incoherencies in this as I see from a religion/culture basis. It does, at least, seem to be out of print, and the new/used vendors are asking insane amounts (from $60 to $200 for a *used* copy and more than $400 for a new one!), which should be enough to dissuade anybody from harboring lingering thoughts of "gee, that could be interesting".

Notes:
1. http://btripp-books.livejournal.com/45549.html
2. http://amzn.to/29OXDNB

Sunday, November 18, 2007[1]

Do go get a copy of this book ...

I've been putting off reading some of my "conservative" books for a while because, despite the refreshing feeling of reading something in the political sphere that I actually *agree* with, the subjects brought up in these tend to depress the hell out of me. I really like Mona Charen's books, as they are *massively* annotated (over 700 source references for a 236-page book), and she, unlike Ann Coulter, never embarrasses with forays into thumping for religion.

A follow-up to her excellent book Useful Idiots[2], which took a look at how the Liberal/Left was complicit in the scourge of totalitarian (primarily those of the Communist bent, of course) states around the globe over the past half century and more, Do-Gooders: How Liberals Hurt Those They Claim to Help (and the Rest of Us)[3] turns its attention to the disaster that Liberal/Left policies have wrought at home, the core concept appearing in this paragraph from the introduction:

> Are liberals truly more concerned about the poorest and weakest members of society than other Americans? Or are they simply in love with the idea of their own righteousness? When you demonstrate indifference to the harmful effects of your supposedly benevolent efforts, isn't it fair to call your motives into question? Besides, throughout the past four decades, liberals have caused real damage. If that is "compassion", then clearly we need a great deal less of it.

I found the bit about "the idea of their own righteousness" a sterling observation, as damn near every Liberal that I have ever known was more into how "they felt" rather than the ultimate effects of what they were doing to create those warm fuzzies!

This book looks at social hot buttons such as law and order, race relations, the rise of the Welfare state, the destruction of the "traditional" family, the root causes of homelessness, and the decay of education. Here's a sample of what she says about the penultimate of those:

> Homelessness came into being because liberal policy makers embraced a series of foolish ideas. They themselves were alienated from society, and so they romanticized the mentally ill and transformed them into social critics. This was unjust both to American society and to the mentally ill themselves, who paid a terrible price for the liberals' social experiment.

Frankly, *most* of the ills discussed in the book can be traced back to "foolish ideas" embraced by self-centered idealists whose basic drive was making themselves look "smart" or "enlightened" to their narrow peer group! However, as small as the Liberal/Left "theoretical core" might have been, they had a HUGE cheering section in the press, especially in the post-Watergate press filled with Quixotic warriors seeking to take down the next Dragon of normalcy, sanity, or tradition. For most of the past 40 years, there has not been a Leftist lie too blatant for the Press to ignore investigating, preferring to grab the falsehood and advance it by any means possible ...

> *The Democrats, of course, can say the moon is a balloon. Without the echo chamber of the press, their words would scarcely ripple the capital's reflecting pool. But the liberal press amplifies and dignifies the Democrats' charges, giving the most partisan and unjustified attacks the patina of statesmanship.*

Needless to say, this is certainly the case today, with the Democratic leadership (and their allies in the media and academia) *daily* spewing out venom with no basis in fact, that goes on to become "common knowledge" among the unquestioning mass that still relies on the Left-controlled MSM:

> *(claiming that "[test scores] don't tell us anything" is) a familiar do-gooder trope. If the facts don't support your point of view, dismiss the facts as irrelevant.*

... after all, who needs facts if your "goals" are pure enough ... can't make an omelet without breaking a few eggs, right? Arrgh! I get enraged just thinking of this.

Anyway, Do-Gooders[4] is *another* of those books that I really wish EVERYBODY would read, but I doubt any Liberals out there would dare to (after all, *their friends* would be *mortified* to know somebody who was reading a "blacklisted" conservative author and would probably freeze them out as a turn-coat for the simple act of considering the evidence!), and I fear it will only raise the bloodpressure of the conservatives. This is, however, available for very little at the moment. Amazon's new/used vendors have the trade paperback available *new* for only 1¢ (an even $4 with shipping), and Amazon has the hardcover at a special bargain price of just $4.99 ... I've been considering buying six (gotta get that free shipping) just to have extra copies to give out! It's still in print, so you can likely even get it through your local brick-and-mortar store, but DO go get a copy, and marvel at the horrors that Liberalism has foisted on our once-great country!

Notes:
1. http://btripp-books.livejournal.com/45668.html
2. http://btripp-books.livejournal.com/39941.html
3-4. http://amzn.to/29IhGxh

Thursday, November 22, 2007[1]

(sigh) ... what to say?

I was surprised at how much *sadness* reading this collection brought up ... especially at the end, of course. This was one of those books that somebody figured would be a good xmas/bday gift for me ... heck, it could have been my Mom ... as I rarely, if ever, buy "sports" books on my own, and (needless to say) it's been sitting around for a few years. Out of the Blue: The Remarkable Story of the 2003 Chicago Cubs[2] is one of those "instant" books churned out by the Chicago Tribune, relying on a vast library of photos, and a platoon of writers close to the team. Frankly, because of their day-to-day familiarity with the subject, these type of books *are* pretty decent chronicles of the events, but they're hardly "high art". However, paging through this was quite the trip down memory lane for this life-long Cubs fan.

For those of you *not* afflicted with the chronic disease of "Cubs Fever", the team won their division in 2003 after a grueling 3-way battle between themselves, St. Louis, and Houston, with the winner not really decided until the last game of the season. They had impressive pitching (Wood, Prior, Zambrano, Clement, etc.) and Sammy Sosa providing offensive pop (yes, that was the "corked bat" controversy season). The post-season first drew a see-saw battle with Atlanta, which the Cubs won 3-2, advancing to the National League Championship Series against Florida, where the Cubs went up 3-1, giving them *three games* to notch one win to make it to the World Series for the first time since the jet engine existed.

Three games to win one. Heck, in game #6, they were up 3-0 in the 8th, with 1 out ... when a lazy fly ball headed to left field and was drifting out of bounds. Moises Alou is following it, glove ready, nearing the wall, a split-second from making it 2 outs in the inning when ... when ... when "IT" happened. The since-notorious Steve Bartman reached out, *right over Alou's glove*, and tried to grab a souvenir. Because the play was over the wall and not over the field, the Umps ruled it wasn't fan interference (although in the pictures, his hand was nearly *in* Alou's glove), so it was simply a foul ball, rather than being 1 out away from being out of the inning. This, obviously, totally shook up the Cubs (Alou was *livid*), and "the wheels came off the cart", Florida scoring *eight runs* and taking the game, and the next, coming back from being down 1-3 on the road.

I had a very busy schedule that week, and had bought a small palm-sized radio to listen to the games while I was out and about. I can still well recall the horrible feeling in my gut as those last three games ticked down. It was a nightmare. Much of this washed back over me reading Out of the Blue[3]. So, unless you're a real masochistic Cubs fan (or a Sox fan looking to relive one of *your* favorite moments), I have a hard time recommending this, despite it being a very good capsule of that season.

Next season is the 100th anniversary of the last time the Cubs won the World Series. A *century* of anguish like this.

Anyway, this *does* still seem to be in print (I guess there are enough White Sox and Cardinals fans out there to keep it moving), but you can get a "good" copy (what, did they change the ending?) for under a buck (before shipping, of course) from the Amazon new/used vendors. (sigh)

Notes:

1. http://btripp-books.livejournal.com/45876.html
2-3. http://amzn.to/29OWq8K

Wednesday, November 28, 2007[1]

Well ...

I'm surprised that I only recently became aware of this book by Hans Li. I was poking around on Amazon, looking at Alberto Villoldo's and Eric Jendresen's books, I believe, when I noted Hans' name in the mix on one. When I clicked through to *his* author page I found The Ancient Ones: Sacred Monuments of the Inka, Maya & Cliffdweller[2] listed, and ordered a used copy. Hans was on many, if not most, of the same trips that I took with Alberto back in the 80's-90's, and I was not aware he'd done a book like this. He is from a very significant Chinese family, with centuries of eastern healing knowledge, and much of his work (such as establishing the Waka Foundation[3]) appears to have been in relation to that grounding ... although he professionally has trained as an architect and photographer.

Obviously, that last piece is what provided the genesis of this book, being a collection of B&W photos from sites in South America, Central America, and the Four Corners region (primarily covering Incan, Mayan, and Anasazi ruins), woven together with texts, both modern and ancient. As I have traveled a good deal in all three of these areas, it was quite a pleasant remembering to see these pictures (I'm guessing that I've been to about half to three-quarters of the ruins shown here), some for rather remarkable things that happened there.

Hans, of course, is not a "disinterested eye" when approaching these subjects either, as he has studied techniques of native healing and spirituality in many of these locations, and that "knowing" aspect hangs over these images, shifting them away from "vacation snaps" or "photo journalism" and into something deeper. Aside from the exclusive use of black and white, there is very little "arting up" of the pictures here, and unlike some books[4] there is no effort made to mystify the places shown, rather Li takes an approach suggesting the eye was simply opening *wider* to take in more of the essence of these sites.

Frankly, many of the ruins pictured will look very familiar because the photos are taken from the same spots as everybody else's pictures ... however, this can't really be faulted, as in most cases (especially in the Cliffdweller sites), there are only certain places where one both is allowed access, and they provide an interesting shot. Of course, the familiarity of knowing how/where a particular picture was snapped helped bring back memories of various places to me stronger than they might have were these taken under "special" circumstances.

As far as the text goes, it is a mixed bag. Parts of this are Hans Li's personal stories, woven in with assorted native myths and writings (there is a lot of the *Popul Vuh* in the Maya section), plus an introduction within the Inca section by Alberto Villoldo. As I've noted in reviews of his recent books, I've been sort of having to re-discover Alberto as he's moved beyond the place he was when I was working with him ... well, this book is a bit like "coming home" as the invocations and general "world sense" in here is "right where I left off", so is somewhat reassuring that I'm not mis-remembering those times. As this is from a dozen and more years back, I wonder what new paths Hans may have taken since putting this out.

The Ancient Ones[5] appears to be out of print (although there still is a web site[6] dedicated to it), but if you're looking for a *deal*, that's not necessarily a bad thing, as Amazon's new/used vendors have "very good" copies of this (originally $35.00 large-format hardcover book) for as little as $5.25 (plus shipping). If you enjoy the archaeology of the Americas, and sincere mystical approaches, this book probably belongs in your library as well.

Notes:

1. http://btripp-books.livejournal.com/46294.html
2. http://amzn.to/29A1EEW
3. http://www.waka.org/
4. http://btripp-books.livejournal.com/37829.html
5. http://amzn.to/29A1EEW
6. http://www.theancient1s.com/

Sunday, December 2, 2007[1]

Skipping ahead here ...

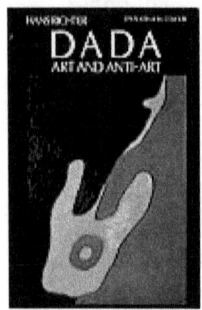

For those following along with my LibraryThing[2] listings, this review is, indeed, out-of-order. I've been waiting to get "the right angle" on my previously-read book, and as this was "fresh in my head", I wanted to get the impressions down before it started to slip away.

This is part of The World Of Art series by Oxford University Press, and I have *no clue* of when or how it found its way into my vast to-be-read collection, but this is a 1978 reprint (so it could have been hanging around since *college*) of a 1965 translation of the 1964 original in German. As such, it *is* rather "dated" ("the future" sub-section of the "Neo-Dada" chapter refers to "happenings" performed in 1962!), but Hans Richter's Dada: Art and Anti-Art[3] is a really remarkable book. Richter had been one of the core group of "Zürich Dada" in 1915-1920, and was on friendly terms with the various later movements in New York, Paris, Berlin, etc., and thereby is very much an eye-witness to a cultural movement which has become legendary.

Divided into sections dealing with the Dada scene as it evolved in various locations, Richter naturally paints the most detailed picture of the initial flowering of the movement, in neutral Switzerland, during the chaos of World War One. Artists from many countries (Richter himself had served in the German army, was wounded and released) found their way to Zürich and began working together in a group which echoed the madness all around them. As he knew the protagonists well here, he is able to bring the artists and actions in Zürich to a particular vividness.

In many other settings, however, he relies on the recall of others, and admits that (in several cases) at the remove from which he was writing (some 30+ years later), the specific details were often hard to determine or a point of contention between various individuals' memories. However, he does do a good job of presenting the "flavor" of the Dada movement in each of its major homes.

Towards the end of the book, the whole "movement" of Dada is placed in an over-all historical context, suggesting that the artists in Zürich, Paris, etc., had taken the tools (and much of the sensibilities) of the Futurists and set them in new directions, only to be wholly swallowed up by Surrealism within a decade, which then itself eventually morphed into what we would consider "pop art" (there is a fascinating recalling of a discussion that Richter had with Roy Lichtenstein about how he came to develop his "comic art" ... which turns out to have evolved in response to Lichtenstein's 8-year-old's reaction to his "abstract" art!).

Dada: Art and Anti-Art[4] was quite a charming read, with the benefits of being partially a personal story (but without much "I, me, we"), in having immediate impressions of the subject, while still being a fairly objective (and reasonably well-researched, as Richter had contacted many of the artists/poets/etc. involved to clarify points and get other feedback) study of the movement. Needless to say, however, when listing "fallen comrades" there was more pathos hanging in the words than would have been noted in the writings of some random art historian.

I was glad to see that this book is still in print (in a 1997 edition[5] from a different publisher), so it should be available through your local brick-and-mortar store. Various used copies are available as well through the usual suspects. The book is, as one would guess, well-illustrated, and is quite a nice introduction to the subject of Dada for anybody that has an interest in these things (and, frankly, reading this has set a little fire going in my head about following up on some long-contemplated art projects!). I would recommend it to anybody wishing to educate themselves on this fascinating period in Western Art & Culture.

Notes:

1. http://btripp-books.livejournal.com/46478.html
2. http://btripp-books.com/
3-5. http://amzn.to/29A19uG

Saturday, December 15, 2007[1]

Still skipping ahead ...

Again, apologies to those (assuming that there might be some) who expect these reviews to follow along with my "collection order" from LibraryThing[2] ... I still haven't gotten around to doing a review of a book I finished a couple of weeks back, but hope to get to it this weekend!

The current read is an odd little book ... I picked it up at the famed Newberry Library Book Fair a year or so back, and for some reason it wanted to get read this month. Delhi and its Neighbourhood[3] is a publication of the Archaeological Survey of India, authored by a Y.D. Sharma back in 1964. The copy I have is a 1982 re-print of the 1974 second edition (which, judging from page count, was a significant expansion on the initial publication).

Although this went to press in 1982, it has that "antique" feel of many books coming out of South Asia ... as the pages are "hand set" (you can see where blocks of type had been swapped out for edits) and the photos are that particular high-contrast B&W which recalls thick metal plates set in wood frames.

It's an odd feeling reading a book like this, both from the noted physical aspects, and the fact that it is, essentially, a tourist guide of various historical and archaeological sites in and around Delhi. The book consists of about 1/3 brief historical over-view of the region, and 2/3 descriptions of locations and features of various sites. Since I am not in Delhi (although I did visit a number of places listed in here when I was in India back in the early 80's), I am left to having the book "paint word pictures for me" mostly, as there are only about 30 photos to cover 150 or so mentioned places. This, of course, would be far less likely were they to do a *Third* edition on modern computer equipment, where the cost of adding photos is simply that of sending somebody out to shoot the images!

As I mentioned, I have a passing familiarity with a dozen or so of the things described here, so it was a bit of a "trip down memory lane" for me in reading it, enough so that I wasn't *totally* frustrated with entries like: *"About 400m south-east of the Flagstaff Tower lies the Chauburji-Masjid, a double-storeyed structure with a central chamber surrounded by a small chamber on each side."* followed by suggestions of what might have been there if the whole thing wasn't all in ruins. Needless to say, *pictures* of each site would have helped a whole lot!

This is not to say that there aren't *fascinating* bits and pieces through the book (such as archaeological traces of cultures in the Delhi area going back to at least 1,000bce, and pretty good indications that Indraprastha, capital of the Pandavas in the *Mahabharata*, was a historical place in the Delhi region. Of course, "archaeological traces" are what you get a lot of in India as the Muslims did a pretty bang-up job of *destroying everything* that they could of the previous Hindu culture, something that I certainly saw in India (mosques built on the foundations of ancient temples), and that is repeatedly referred to in the descriptions here (where materials looted from Hindu structures were re-used in Islamic architecture). Another notable "theme" is that in a lot of cases there are tombs, but no clear idea (aside from fanciful local namings) of whose tombs these were. I guess the Islamic culture's phobias for "representations" must have extended into "iffy" record keeping (or inscriptions ... needless to say, the ancient Egyptians, death cultists *extraordinares*, would be mystified at building a tomb that didn't preserve the deceased's *name* for all eternity!). Despite this, familiar names do crop up (to those with some background in Indian history), lending a bit of familiarity with some of the text.

The book also comes with two fold-out maps, one being an over-view of the region with the various "cities" (each new conqueror seemed to start their own in the area), and one a detailed plan of the famed Red Fort.

Obviously, I think that Delhi and its Neighbourhood[4] would be *greatly* improved by having a new edition with lots of pictures ... *that* would be an interesting "armchair traveler" read for anybody. As it currently stands, however, I think it would be somewhat impenetrable for somebody without at least a moderate knowledge of the area. Not that getting a copy is a high likelihood at this point, with only *two* copies in play with the Amazon new/used vendors (I guess I was lucky to stumble over one). It is, however, out there if this sounds like something that you need to add to your library!

Notes:

1. http://btripp-books.livejournal.com/46676.html
2. http://btripp-books.com/
3-4. http://amzn.to/29w99MK

Saturday, December 15, 2007[1]

"The earth is all conceivable pain compacted into a single point."

This was, at least, a fast read. I had *really wanted* to like this book, being as it is the first of the "Early Reviewers" program releases from LibraryThing[2] that I've managed to snag. But, frankly, my #1 take-away from reading Christopher Spranger's The Comedy of Agony: A Book of Poisonous Contemplations[3] was wondering how it managed to get published at all! I at first went to check to see if Leaping Dog Press was a "vanity press" through which Spranger had put out this book, but it appears that this is not the case ... they define themselves, however, thusly: "Leaping Dog Press and Asylum Arts Press publish accessible, edgy, witty, and challenging contemporary poetry, fiction, and works in translation, with Asylum Arts Press having an additional focus on surrealism and the avant garde." ... now, back when I was in the small publishing biz, I was certainly guilty of putting out works that perhaps appealed more to me, personally, than to any particular audience (and our sales showed this), so it is possible that Spranger is a friend of the editors, or a "favorite flavor" that they decided to go to press with that I, at least, do not find appealing at all.

Now, those who know me, or have read much of my own writing, would rather expect that I would connect with Spranger's brand of nihilism. This book is, if nothing else, unredeemed negativity cover-to-cover, and I've certainly "been there" myself. However, my reaction to the prose here is somewhat akin to being harangued by a smelly bum (oddly enough, the very subject of one of his stories) ranting on about some paranoid theory that just happens to come close to some secretly-held political view of one's own. You recognize the congruent theme, but do wish it wasn't in such a crazy and malodorous package!

As to the package ... the book is mercifully brief at 140 pages, with the first half being three sections of assorted "aphorisms" and the second a couple of dozen "commentaries" running from a half to five pages. There are some high points, some arch barbs that strike their targets dead on, but also material that seems "unedited" and somewhat flat, passages which could have been easily made *better* with some basic effort. I believe the author has the *skills* necessary for this (as there were many quite well-crafted phrases through the book), but not the intent.

These thoughts led me to my second *"Hmmmmm..."* moment of the book, as the failings, both literary and philosophical, were so blatant that it made me wonder if the entire exercise wasn't some "Discordian working". After all, there is a rather detailed bit of text (appearing on the back cover, as well in the promotional materials for the book) which pretty much sets up the book's original intents with some lofty goal of re-visioning Dante yet admitting going nowhere close to where that would have been. Thus this being the book which isn't the book that would have been the book had this book been the book that was initially intended to be the book ... sounds mighty Erisian to me!

As far as what's on the pages, it's all about pain, and horror, and fear, and loss, and sadness, and God and the Devil, and the Reality of Being ... none of which is pretty. I'll share some choicer bits with you here, these from the first part of the book:

> "There is no scream of horror that could not be mistaken for an *exact description* of the universe."
>
> "Only in our most violent fits of self-loathing do we get a glimpse of what it must feel like to be God."
>
> "History is a catastrophe *in progress*."
>
> "Life is a question of intensity, not of time. A tortured poet lives more in twenty seconds than the rest of us do in twenty years."
>
> "Supposing this life to be some kind of undisclosed intelligence test, I doubt any but suicides are getting passing grades."

And these from the later section:

> (from *Stoicism's Mistake*) "... Aware that man does not desire to escape pain but to stuff himself full of it, the Christians took a more sensible approach. ... Going to any lengths to gratify our weakness for the Worst, they made masochism into a virtue and martyrdom into a goal. And for the grand finale, they decided to represent their *god* as crucified: a brilliant marketing strategy ..."
>
> (from *The Unconquerable?*) "... A manmade catastrophe could wipe out every creature on the face of the earth, effectively putting an end to the scourge of reproduction, but it doubtful if even then life would admit defeat. In fact she'd probably scarcely take notice. Who cannot envision her, one hundred years after this supreme devastation, creeping through some crack and comporting herself as if nothing at all had occurred?"

As you can see, there is a wry tone operating here which, combined with the stated (and notably unapproached) aims of the book, place the entire project into a realm more in the Discordian or Sub-Genius type than the Hell that Spranger nominally sees all existence being.

If there were any one thing to recommend this book, it would be the piece entitled *The Unenlightened* which should be required reading for anybody who has ever studied Eastern religion/philosophy/metaphysics! Positing that those of us still extant are simply the dullest of the dull, relating to the author's own bothersome embodiment, it would be well worth quoting in its entirety here, but I won't for length, as well as to give you a reason to at least pick up a copy to page through (91) when you're next at a bookstore.

Being that this is a new book, it will likely be at the bigger brick-and-mortar stores. If you feel like thrashing about in some oddly-framed nihilist goo, you could get this on-line as well, it's 22% off cover via Amazon, and is already available at a considerable discount from their new/used vendors. I really can't recommend this, but if being stuck in a car with a bitter, suicidal, yet still-funny friend sounds like a swell way of spending a couple of hours, this might be something you'd enjoy.

Notes:

1. http://btripp-books.livejournal.com/46868.html
2. http://btripp-books.com/
3. http://amzn.to/29zZRQa

Thursday, December 20, 2007[1]

Ninjas! ...

So, I was digging through some old boxes of "to be read" books, and looking for something to "take up the slack" at home while I finish reading that 800-page monster I'm in the midst of whilst on the train to and from work. And there it was, Secrets Of The Ninja[2] by Ashida Kim. At a scant 152 pages, it wasn't threatening to drag into the new year (especially given that it's about half photos), so I pulled it out of its literary limbo and into the current reading mix.

Frankly, I was quite surprised to see (when logging it into my LibraryThing[3] catalog) that there is a "new" edition of this (2000 vs. 1981) and I wonder if they shot new pictures. As noted above, this is extensively illustrated (200 photos and diagrams), but most of the shots are "so 1981", looking like production stills on a grade-D kung fu movie from the era ... giving the book, a quarter century later, an almost comical air. Of course, with 200 illustrations spread out over not quite 152 pages (discounting a half dozen blanks for chapter pagination), this leaves what amounts to a brief "pamphlet" of actual text.

However, as much as I might have approached this in a belittling manner, the material is very focused, and deadly serious, and seems to be legitimately attempting to encapsulate a dozen or more years of training into a book that could realistically be blown through in an afternoon.

The first quarter of the book is dedicated to preparatory exercises and a process of meditations, mind-focusing hand grips, and various "hypnotizing" hand movements (primarily tracing out certain Chinese characters while the hands are locked in a particular manner). It is off-handedly noted that these preparations are likely to take many years before the student is ready for any of the "practical" instruction later in the book ... yet I wonder how many of its readers pay any attention to that particular caveat.

The remainder of the book is sort of "what a Ninja should know" in various contexts, with 14 chapters covering everything from "The Art Of Hiding" to "Leaving No Trace". In between these, however, is a *whole lot of killing*. Ninjas, of course, "don't mess around", and most of these instructions deal with death blows, where, how, and what time one should expect to have to wait for unconsciousness and death. Details are given on how to surprise guards, how to escape from arrest, and how to wreak bloody havoc with throwing stars, nunchakus, short swords, garrotes, and even sand and dirt!

By the time I got done reading about all the ways of crushing parts of the skull, severing assorted arteries, snapping the neck, and breaking the spine, I became rather worried about how *fragile* the human body might be ... after all, most of the moves illustrated are not too far off from what is seen on your average wrestling broadcast (especially the spine-breaking moves), that it made me wonder just how much actual *force* is required for these to be harmful, with the very similar images creating a great degree of cognitive dissonance!

Again, most of this is very straight forward ... do this to kill your opponent in this situation, do that to kill your opponent in this other situation, etc. ... however, it did, on rare occasion, drift into almost a philosophical mode, with this bit striking me as particularly choice:

> *Keep the door on your right.* This is advise from Miaymoto Musashi, who fought over two hundred duels and died of old age; it is not likely he was wrong.

... this in a discussion of "facing multiple adversaries". Practical data, if nearly into the micro-management zone (one wonders just what sort of a study could be crafted to determine *why* keeping the door to one's right is such a good idea).

If you feel like a quick read on meditation & carnage, this is, as noted, still in print so *could* be purchased from your local brick & mortar book store while the cashier snickered at you, but I'm sure it would be more comfortably obtained on-line, and Amazon's new/used vendors have "like new" copies for under a buck, were you to be so inclined. Me, I'm sort of glad to have read it (just in case I need to efficiently dispatch some latter-day Samurai on the subway), but oddly creeped out by it all the same!

Notes:

1. http://btripp-books.livejournal.com/47352.html
2. http://amzn.to/29zZOnt
3. http://btripp-books.com/

Tuesday, December 25, 2007[1]

Ho, ho, ho ...

OK, so the *cynical* out there might posit that I waited for Xmas to get around to reviewing Richard Dawkins' The God Delusion[2], but it's really not that way. While it is true that I've had this *sitting around* for four weeks since I got done reading it (and have finished and reviewed several books in the interim), I really haven't been "saving it" for a seasonal broadside. No, the truth of the matter was that I was catching up on some organizational things today, and had cleared "to be read" books off of a shelf, making it ready for the last 30-40 books I've read ... as it turned out, this just made that shelf, so I was really *forced* to get around to writing about it.

Now, regular readers of my journal will recall that I recently posted my "angst" over this ... I really prefer not to spark "flame wars" with my reviews, but so many of my *conservative* readers are of a religious bent, and so many of my *non-religious* readers are of a *leftist* bent, that I can hardly avoid a certain level of ugliness, being one of those odd "anti-religion" conservative folks who can't seem to help but offend *everybody*.

Anyway. Don't mistake the delay in the review for not wanting to *rave* about The God Delusion[3], as I really feel that Dawkins hit a home run with this. Avoiding many of the pit-falls that I've noted in other similar books, Dawkins not only picks apart religion point-for-point, but also slogs into the standard counter-arguments relied on by the faithful. From clearly showing that Einstein was a non-believer to establishing that Hitler considered himself a "good Catholic" (despite having a great deal of disdain for religion for coddling "the weak"), many theistic straw men are torn down. Once again, I have put *way* too many scraps of paper in a book, which would (were I to dig out "the really good parts") make this review go on for pages and pages.

Dawkins did a wonderful job with the structure of the book, at first looking at what might lie behind religion, in "A Deeply Religious Non-Believer", where he sketches out that the feeling of awe and wonder that an atheistic scientist experiences when trying to make sense of the enormity and complexity of the universe is *a religious feeling*, but it is not a *supernatural* religious feeling. One can experience the connection with "things larger than oneself" without turning off the mind and freezing one's world-view in some bronze-age mythos! He then walks through the development of religions in "The God Hypothesis", where polytheism cedes to monotheism, and how ill-based on *reality* nearly all manifestations of "religious doctrine" are. Dawkins then looks to the other side, presenting a chapter on "Arguments for God's Existence", and fairly easily knocks these aside, leading to "Why There Almost Certainly Is No God" where a wide array of logical, scientific, and historical evidence plays against the hypothesis of a "typical" (i.e. *supernatural*) God.

At this point Dawkins returns to his main area of expertise, and takes a look at "The Roots of Religion" ... why *is* there religion? From very early on these patterns have been with us, what good do they serve? On the way to answering these questions he moves to another... "The Roots of Morality: Why Are We Good?" ... much has been written on this topic in context of logic games such as "the prisoner's dilemma", and it come out that your average human being is reasonably "good" most of the time simply because it's a better "strategy" for a social animal. This does bring up the question of *why* so many "religious" people outright assume that if you do not "go to church" (especially whatever brand it is that *they* go to), you can not possibly be *moral*, with the rather ugly implication that these religion-blinded folks implicitly assume that if they did *not* have their regular indoctrination sessions they would be killing, raping, and pillaging. Personally, looking at places in the world where religion has a strong hand, there may be something there ... but only in the case of *religious people* being unleashed on their unsuspecting neighbors!

Here is where "it gets good". First Dawkins looks at "The 'Good' Book and the Changing Moral *Zeitgeist*" of how much "cherry picking" modern monotheists indulge in to allow themselves to tip-toe around the ugly sadistic mess that are their "holy books". In this section he also addresses the question of Hitler and Stalin and Mao, who, while arguably (or nominally) atheistic, were actually "popes" of religions of the state or religions of the Leader. In none of these cases was there the rational discourse of the scientific atheist, but the emotion-driven passion for the "in group" and devotion to a Leader or a State indistinguishable from "religion". The next chapter, "What's Wrong With Religion? Why Are We So Hostile?" looks at the predictable, *unavoidable* ways that religion perverts everything it touches, from "Fundamentalism and the subversion of science" (a sub-chapter heading) to "How 'moderation' in faith fosters fanaticism" (another). Where faith is, reason is not, or is in such a convoluted distortion of itself that it is slave to the dark aspects of faith. One of the darkest, is how religion systematically destroys children, this is one of Dawkins' on-going themes and in "Childhood, Abuse, and the Escape from Religion" he walks the reader through the nightmare scenario that 90% of the world accepts as "business as usual".

Frankly, at this point, I would have liked to have seen Dawkins go on a red-faced, busting blood vessels, anti-religion rant ... but wouldn't that have been the *religious* way of closing? Rather, he goes into "A Much Needed Gap?" which starts off dealing with the "God of the gaps" idea (basically the "if we can't explain it ... it must be GOD!" sort of twaddle) and closes with a delightful "thought experiment" called "The mother of all burkas" (another sub-heading), which points out that we, as creatures evolved in the "Middle World", the place of rocks, and trees, and clouds and predictable slow-moving "stuff" can't fully "get" the micro-cosmic or the macro-cosmic, unless we approach it from a scientific viewpoint. The religious viewpoint is viewing the whole amazing universe through that little eye-slit in the burka, and saying "this is how things are, there is nothing beyond the human-scale, so if it is, it's the work of some image of ourself that we call God" (my paraphrase, not Dawkins' words). Which really puts in context how small and pitiful the religious world-view is in relation to the awe and wonder of a scientific, atheistic approach to the universe.

Needless to say, this is one of those "Everybody Needs To Read This!!!" books. It's in your local brick-and-mortar store, but Amazon has it for more than a third off of cover. Anybody with doubts about religion (or on-going irritation with the Religious) really *really* ought to read The God Delusion[4], and those of you who still cling to your narrow-band imaginary friends, this one should open your eyes to why the rest of us think you may be dangerous, and are certainly in the grip of an unnecessary "delusion".

Notes:

1. http://btripp-books.livejournal.com/47525.html

2-4. http://amzn.to/29qgN8E

Saturday, December 29, 2007[1]

Long time for this one ...

As noted in my last review, I just got a shelf's worth of books "filed" from what I've been reading, and in the process, had to move the stacks of "to be read" books *from* that shelf and into storage boxes (I now have *five* such storage boxes around my desk here, aside from the "more active" to-be-read piles sitting out). One of the books that had been languishing on that shelf was Bob Stewart and John Matthews' Legendary Britain: An Illustrated Journey[2] ... I say "languishing" because when I got into it, I found it inscribed with a note from some friends, obviously being a wedding present, and, as our 16th anniversary was just a week ago, I guess it took me a full sixteen years to "get around to reading this"! I suspect that the main reason that I was never quite able to "pull the trigger" on getting into this one was that it was sort of hard to approach, being something of a "mash-up" between different genres, an archaeological travel guide, a history book, a book about legends, a book *of* legends (albeit re-constructed from multiple sources), and a book that combined maps and photographs of various sites with "kiddie book" illustrations to go with the tales. I guess every time I was interested in reading *one* of those elements, the rest just didn't appeal to me, but this past week it was "something different" so made it into the reading mix.

I take it (both from references in the book and poking around on Amazon) that the authors have written quite a bit about ancient British mythic themes, of the Land, Kingship, and the Under/Otherworld, and these weave through Legendary Britain[3], freely mixing with "historical" material and analysis of surviving legends and other cultural traces, giving it almost a "dream-like" take-away, as history and myth and legend and places and names all blur in this particular telling.

As one would guess by its sub-title "An Illustrated Journey", this is a progression through various British sites, from Cornwall in the south up to the Orkneys in the far north, making 10 stops along the way, chosen more for their thematic elements of Prophecy, Kingship, and the Land, than for their fame as archaeological zones. For instance, Stonehenge is skipped over, and Avebury only mentioned in relation to other sites, yet Bath has its own chapter.

Characters from the legends, Arthur (along with relatives and associates), Robin Hood (with others), Merlin in his various forms, Tristan & Isolde, and various denizens of the Under/Otherworld, most notably the Fairy Queen, are the main element here, weaving in and out of the "historical" and evolving as the re-telling of centuries passed. Each chapter ends with a "legend" re-imaged by the authors, be it of The Smith King of Wayland's Smithy or of an ancient hermit of Iona, which brings together bits and pieces from mythic remnants, historical elements, and archaeological contexts.

Of course, this stuff is rather "hereditary" to me, so I get a serious hankering to visit these sites when I read this sort of material (I had a couple of books as a wee lad which dealt with visits to the Faerie Realm which touched me deeply), but "your mileage may vary". I'm not sure how coherent this book would be for one who had *not* had at least a general familiarity with the long-view history of the British Isles, and the archaeological remains and legends of the culture. If one only knows the "Disney" versions of Robin Hood or King Arthur, one might be rather confused at the elements introduced here!

Legendary Britain[4] is, however, a rather unique book and is delightful within the strange context it creates for itself, while "neither this, neither that" as far as the component parts, it does pull together a particular telling, which it stays true to all the way through. Currently out of print, this hardcover is available via the Amazon new/used vendors fairly reasonably with a "good" copy going for just over $4 and a "new" copy going for just under $8 (both of those plus shipping, of course), so if this sounds like a literary journey that you'd like to make, it's available.

Notes:

1. http://btripp-books.livejournal.com/47838.html
2-4. http://amzn.to/29Z3kG5

Monday, January 31, 2007[1]

A grim read ...

The most remarkable thing about this book is that it was written by two reporters from *The New York Times* (Judith Miller and Stephen Engelberg) and an editor from *The Oregonian* (William Broad) ... if ever there was a team that one would suspect of hard-Left spin, it would be a combination like that, and yet (except for a bit at the very end) there is little, if any, evident Liberal Bias. Needless to say, a title like Germs: Biological Weapons and America's Secret War[2] sets one up to expect one of those Marxist-inspired screeds against the USA's "military-industrial complex", but the thrust of the book would have been better presented with a subtitle along the lines of "how our trusting nature got us into trouble again". I suspect that the phrase "America's Secret War" is only on the cover to get the Che t-shirt crowd to buy it ... as the core thesis is more about how we spent a quarter century *not* fighting a war that nearly all our opponents were deeply engaged in.

While Germs[3] is not a historical over-view per se of America's experience with biowarfare agents, it does paint a fairly full picture of that, if having much of the "historical" material in background and asides to the specific events and characters being detailed. It is noted that the U.S. swore off all bio-agent work in Richard Nixon's 1969 announcement, and was a key signatory (and one could argue, solitary actual *participant*) to the 1972 Biological and Toxins Weapons Convention, a bit of diplomacy on the par with Neville Chamberlain's that put our ability to recognize and react to biowar incidents (let alone *retaliate*) far behind our traditional foes, and even many 2nd and 3rd world regimes.

The book starts out with a little-known story, that of the "bioterror" efforts of the Rajneesh followers to attack local residents who opposed their huge compound in Oregon back in 1984 and 1985. At the time it was thought best to cover up the story, so as to not cause "copycat" attacks, which in this case primarily involved introducing Salmonella into salad bars in surrounding communities. One thing that this scenario made very clear was that the U.S. was almost *totally blind* to the use of bio agents, and the investigation went on a considerable time before it dawned on authorities that these had been deliberate attacks. Not only had there not been a "mental model" that this was a possibility, there was virtually no infrastructure to support an investigation.

The book continues with a look at the few people in government, who had been part of the pre-1969 germ programs, and how they were trying to keep some aspects of preparedness available. This then spins into the "cracks in the wall" of the Soviet's *massive* bio-weapon build up, as shown by news leaking out of major "accidents" and a number of key defections. When I say "massive", the USSR was producing *5,000 times* the amount of germ agents that the U.S. was (and had aggressive programs in things like Small Pox and Bubonic Plague that we weren't even messing with) back before '69 ... and they really hadn't pulled back any despite the '72 convention!

When I noted that I was surprised that this book came from the people it did, that is largely due to the next part, detailing just what Saddam had in Iraq. Obviously, *today* the Times would NEVER allow their reporters to vary from the "party line" that there were no WMD in Iraq, yet here are very specific trails of what germs (as well as when, how, and to a certain extent *where*) the Hussein regime had acquired or developed, and the grim scenarios that our military was having to deal with in the months leading up to Desert Storm, where it was fully expected that the Iraqis would use these agents on our troops. There is also some conjectures that "Gulf War Syndrome" is largely due to the destruction of a number of Saddam's ammo depots, and the inadvertent release of bio agents from munitions stored there!

About 1/3rd of the book is a paean to the Clinton administration, describing how it engaged the threat. It appears that Bill Clinton took the bio-war scenario very seriously, and tried to get a structure started for dealing with this. Unfortunately, after so many years "out of the game", this became a project with no "home" and no "core constituents", and the responsibility for bio preparedness is spread out over a dozen or so competing and uncooperative government bureaucracies. This was, of course, driven home by the 2002 anthrax attacks in Washington and Florida, where it took weeks to recognize the "accidental" infections (of mail handlers, etc.), and then dealing with the various copy-cat "hoaxes" that followed (I guess there was something to the Oregon response after all), including an envelope filled with baby powder that one of the authors opened at their desk!

Germs[4] paints a very grim picture of the future, as we are simply *not* prepared to deal with this sort of an attack, and our enemies are quite capable of delivering one. If you're interested in finding out just how dire this situation is, the book is still in print (so could be obtained from your local brick & mortar book vendor), but Amazon's new/used guys currently have "like new" copies of *both* this paperback *and* the hardcover for a penny (an even $4 with shipping), so that would certainly be the way to go. Again, it's a grim, yet engaging, read ... but it is definitely a subject that more people need to know about.

Notes:

1. http://btripp-books.livejournal.com/48094.html

2-4. http://amzn.to/29wD3zn

QR code links
to the
on-line reviews:

Bias: A CBS Insider
Exposes How the Media Distort the News
by
Bernard Goldberg

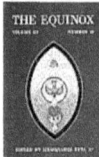

The Equinox, Volume III, Number 10
by
Aleister Crowley / Hymenaeus Beta X°

Shabono: A Visit to a Remote and Magical
World in the South American Rain Forest
by
Florinda Donner

The Wheel of Time:
The Kalachakra in Context
by
Geshe Lhundub Sopa

Kalacakra Tantra
by
Geshe Ngawang Dhargyey

Black Holes and Time Warps:
Einstein's Outrageous Legacy
by
Kip Thorne

The Practice of Kalachakra
by
Glenn H. Mullin

Freedom In Exile:
the Autobiography of the Dalai Lama
by
His Holiness the Dalai Lama

Tibet: The Sacred Realm -
Photographs 1880-1950
by
Lobsang P. Lhalungpa

Mountains of the Middle Kingdom:
Exploring the High Peaks of China and Tibet
by
Galen Rowell

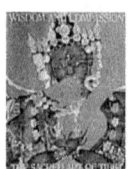

Wisdom and Compassion:
The Sacred Art of Tibet
by
Marylin M. Rhie & Robert A. F. Thurman

Healing and the Mind
by
Bill Moyers

The Monuments of Mars:
a City On the Edge Of Forever
by
Richard C. Hoagland

Might is Right:
The Survival of the Fittest
by
Ragnar Redbeard

The Andean Codex:
Adventures and Initiations
Among the Peruvian Shamans
by
J.E. Williams

The Wheel of Time: The Shamans of Ancient Mexico,
Their Thoughts About Life, Death and the Universe
by
Carlos Castaneda

The Active Side of Infinity
by
Carlos Castaneda

Magical Passes:
The Practical Wisdom
of the Shamans of Ancient Mexico
by
Carlos Castaneda

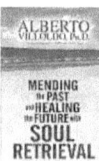

Mending The Past And Healing The Future
with Soul Retrieval
by
Alberto Villoldo

Hypnosis:
How to Put a Smile on Your Face
and Money in Your Pocket
by
Shelley Stockwell

The Demon-Haunted World:
Science as a Candle in the Dark
by
Carl Sagan

Moral Minority:
Our Skeptical Founding Fathers
by
Brooke Allen

The Secret
by
Rhonda Byrne

The Four Agreements:
A Practical Guide to Personal Freedom,
A Toltec Wisdom Book
by
don Miguel Ruiz

Creating Money:
Keys to Abundance
by
Sanaya Roman & Duane Packer

The Power of Now:
A Guide to Spiritual Enlightenment
by
Eckhart Tolle

Spirit & Reason:
The Vine Deloria, Jr., Reader
by
Vine Deloria, Jr.

The Power of Intention:
Learning to Co-create Your World Your Way
by
Dr. Wayne W. Dyer

Fearless Living:
Live without Excuses and Love without Regret
by
Rhonda Britten

Careers for New Agers & Other Cosmic Types
by
Blythe Camenson

The Law of Attraction:
The Basics of the Teachings of Abraham
by
Esther & Jerry Hicks

Letters to a Young Contrarian
by
Christopher Hitchens

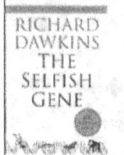

The Selfish Gene
by
Richard Dawkins

The Mind's Sky:
Human Intelligence in a Cosmic Context
by
Timothy Ferris

Libertarianism In One Lesson
by
David Bergland

Art & Physics:
Parallel Visions in Space, Time, and Light
by
Leonard Shlain

The 21 Indispensable Qualities of a Leader:
Becoming the Person Others Will Want to Follow
by
John C. Maxwell

Who's Looking Out for You?
by
Bill O'Reilly

Mayan Vision Quest:
Mystical Initiation in Mesoamerica
by
Cynthia MacAdams, Hunbartz Men
& Charles Bensinger

Sacred Journeys:
An Illustrated Guide to Pilgrimages Around the World
by
Jennifer Westwood

Gurdjieff: An Introduction to His Life and Ideas
by
John Shirley

The Jesus Dynasty:
The Hidden History of Jesus,
His Royal Family, and the Birth of Christianity
by
James D. Tabor

Real Success Without a Real Job:
There Is No Life Like It!
by
Ernie Zelinski

The Cosmic Landscape:
String Theory and the Illusion of Intelligent Design
by
Leonard Susskind

The Englishman's Handbook
by
Idries Shah

The 100 Simple Secrets of Happy People:
What Scientists Have Learned
and How You Can Use It
by
David Niven, Ph.D.

A Devil's Chaplain:
Reflections on Hope, Lies, Science, and Love
by
Richard Dawkins

Useful Idiots:
How Liberals Got It Wrong in the Cold War
and Still Blame America First
by
Mona Charen

Mind Sights: Original Visual Illusions, Ambiguities,
and Other Anomalies, With a Commentary
on the Play of Mind in Perception and Art
by
Roger N. Shepard

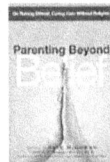

Parenting Beyond Belief:
On Raising Ethical, Caring Kids Without Religion
by
Dale McGowan

The Whole Shebang:
A State-of-the-Universe(s) Report
by
Timothy Ferris

Thoreau: A Book of Quotations
by
Henry David Thoreau

The Ballad of Reading Gaol
and Other Poems
by
Oscar Wilde

Great Speeches by Native Americans
by
Bob Blaisdell, Ed.

The Genealogy of Morals
by
Friedrich Nietzsche

Beowulf
by
R. K. Gordon, Trans.

Chicago Then And Now
by
Elizabeth McNulty

The Nibelungenlied
by
D.G. Mowatt, Trans.

The Constitution of the United States
with the Declaration of Independence
and the Articles of Confederation
by
R.B. Bernstein, Intro.

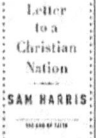

Letter to a Christian Nation
by
Sam Harris

McIlhenny's Gold:
How a Louisiana Family Built the Tabasco Empire
by
Jeffrey Rothfeder

Common Sense, The Rights of Man
and Other Essential Writings of Thomas Paine
by
Thomas Paine

If Democrats Had Any Brains,
They'd Be Republicans
by
Ann Coulter

From Clocks to Chaos: The Rhythms of Life
by
Leon Glass & Michael C. Mackey

Dawn Behind the Dawn:
A Search for the Earthly Paradise
by
Geoffrey Ashe

The Four Insights:
Wisdom, Power, and Grace of the Earthkeepers
by
Alberto Villoldo

The End of Faith:
Religion, Terror, and the Future of Reason
by
Sam Harris

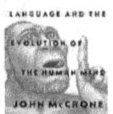

The Ape That Spoke:
Language and the Evolution of the Human Mind
by
John McCrone

Myth of Invariance:
The Origins of the Gods, Mathematics
and Music from the Rg Veda to Plato
by
Ernest G. McClain

Do-Gooders:
How Liberals Hurt Those They
Claim to Help (and the Rest of Us)
by
Mona Charen

Out of the Blue:
The Remarkable Story of the 2003 Chicago Cubs
by
Chicago Tribune

The Ancient Ones:
Sacred Monuments of the Inka, Maya & Cliffdweller
by
Hans Li

Dada: Art and Anti-Art
by
Hans Richter

Delhi and its Neighbourhood
by
Y.D. Sharma

The Comedy of Agony:
A Book of Poisonous Contemplations
by
Christopher Spranger

Secrets Of The Ninja
by
Ashida Kim

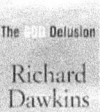

The God Delusion
by
Richard Dawkins

Legendary Britain: An Illustrated Journey
by
Bob Stewart & John Matthews

Germs: Biological Weapons
and America's Secret War
by
Judith Miller, Stephen Engelberg & William Broad

CONTENTS - ALPHABETICAL BY AUTHOR

Brooke Allen — page 41
Moral Minority: Our Skeptical Founding Fathers

Geoffrey Ashe — page 123
*Dawn Behind the Dawn:
A Search for the Earthly Paradise*

David Bergland — page 65
Libertarianism In One Lesson

R.B. Bernstein, Intro. — page 109
*The Constitution of the United States
with the Declaration of Independence
and the Articles of Confederation*

Bob Blaisdell, Ed. — page 100
Great Speeches by Native Americans

Rhonda Britten — page 54
*Fearless Living:
Live without Excuses and Love without Regret*

Rhonda Byrne — page 43
The Secret

Blythe Camenson — page 56
Careers for New Agers & Other Cosmic Types

Carlos Castaneda — page 30
The Active Side of Infinity

Carlos Castaneda	page	32

*Magical Passes: The Practical Wisdom
of the Shamans of Ancient Mexico*

Carlos Castaneda	page	28

*The Wheel of Time: The Shamans of Ancient Mexico,
Their Thoughts About Life, Death and the Universe*

Mona Charen	page	134

*Do-Gooders: How Liberals Hurt Those
They Claim to Help (and the Rest of Us)*

Mona Charen	page	88

*Useful Idiots: How Liberals Got It Wrong
in the Cold War and Still Blame America First*

Ann Coulter	page	119

If Democrats Had Any Brains, They'd Be Republicans

Aleister Crowley / Hymenaeus Beta X°	page	3

The Equinox, Volume III, Number 10

His Holiness the Dalai Lama	page	13

*Freedom In Exile:
the Autobiography of the Dalai Lama*

Richard Dawkins	page	86

*A Devil's Chaplain:
Reflections on Hope, Lies, Science, and Love*

Richard Dawkins	page	149

The God Delusion

Richard Dawkins	page	61

The Selfish Gene

Vine Deloria, Jr.   page 51
    Spirit & Reason: The Vine Deloria, Jr. Reader

Geshe Ngawang Dhargyey   page 8
    Kalacakra Tantra

Florinda Donner   page 4
    Shabono: A Visit to a Remote and Magical World in the South American Rain Forest

Dr. Wayne W. Dyer   page 52
    The Power of Intention: Learning to Co-create Your World Your Way

Timothy Ferris   page 63
    The Mind's Sky: Human Intelligence in a Cosmic Context

Timothy Ferris   page 94
    The Whole Shebang: A State-of-the-Universe(s) Report

Leon Glass & Michael C. Mackey   page 121
    From Clocks to Chaos: The Rhythms of Life

Bernard Goldberg   page 1
    Bias: A CBS Insider Exposes How the Media Distort the News

R. K. Gordon, Trans.   page 104
    Beowulf

Sam Harris   page 128
    The End of Faith: Religion, Terror, and the Future of Reason

Sam Harris — page 111
Letter to a Christian Nation

Esther & Jerry Hicks — page 57
The Law of Attraction:
The Basics of the Teachings of Abraham

Christopher Hitchens — page 59
Letters to a Young Contrarian

Richard C. Hoagland — page 22
The Monuments of Mars:
a City On the Edge Of Forever

Ashida Kim — page 147
Secrets Of The Ninja

Lobsang P. Lhalungpa — page 15
Tibet: The Sacred Realm - Photographs 1880-1950

Hans Li — page 138
The Ancient Ones:
Sacred Monuments of the Inka, Maya & Cliffdweller

Cynthia MacAdams, Hunbartz Men & Charles Bensinger — page 72
Mayan Vision Quest:
Mystical Initiation in Mesoamerica

John C. Maxwell — page 69
The 21 Indispensable Qualities of a Leader:
Becoming the Person Others Will Want to Follow

Ernest G. McClain — page 132
Myth of Invariance: The Origins of the Gods,
Mathematics and Music from the Rg Veda to Plato

John McCrone	page 130
The Ape That Spoke: *Language and the Evolution of the Human Mind*	
Dale McGowan	page 92
Parenting Beyond Belief: *On Raising Ethical, Caring Kids Without Religion*	
Elizabeth McNulty	page 106
Chicago Then And Now	
Judith Miller, Stephen Engelberg & William Broad	page 154
Germs: Biological Weapons and America's Secret War	
D.G. Mowatt, Trans.	page 107
The Nibelungenlied	
Bill Moyers	page 20
Healing and the Mind	
Glenn H. Mullin	page 11
The Practice of Kalachakra	
Friedrich Nietzsche	page 102
The Genealogy of Morals	
David Niven, Ph.D.	page 85
The 100 Simple Secrets of Happy People: *What Scientists Have Learned and How You Can Use It*	
Bill O'Reilly	page 70
Who's Looking Out for You?	
Thomas Paine	page 116
Common Sense, The Rights of Man and *Other Essential Writings of Thomas Paine*	

Ragnar Redbeard   page   24
    Might is Right: The Survival of the Fittest

Marylin M. Rhie & Robert A. F. Thurman   page   19
    Wisdom and Compassion: The Sacred Art of Tibet

Hans Richter   page   140
    Dada: Art and Anti-Art

Sanaya Roman & Duane Packer   page   47
    Creating Money: Keys to Abundance

Jeffrey Rothfeder   page   114
    McIlhenny's Gold:
    How a Louisiana Family Built the Tabasco Empire

Galen Rowell   page   17
    Mountains of the Middle Kingdom:
    Exploring the High Peaks of China and Tibet

don Miguel Ruiz   page   45
    The Four Agreements:
    A Practical Guide to Personal Freedom,
    A Toltec Wisdom Book

Carl Sagan   page   39
    The Demon-Haunted World:
    Science as a Candle in the Dark

Idries Shah   page   83
    The Englishman's Handbook

Y.D. Sharma   page   142
    Delhi and its Neighbourhood

Roger N. Shepard — page 90
Mind Sights: Original Visual Illusions, Ambiguities, and Other Anomalies, With a Commentary on the Play of Mind in Perception and Art

John Shirley — page 75
Gurdjieff: An Introduction to His Life and Ideas

Leonard Shlain — page 67
Art & Physics: Parallel Visions in Space, Time, and Light

Geshe Lhundub Sopa — page 6
The Wheel of Time: The Kalachakra in Context

Christopher Spranger — page 144
The Comedy of Agony: A Book of Poisonous Contemplations

Bob Stewart & John Matthews — page 152
Legendary Britain: An Illustrated Journey

Shelley Stockwell — page 37
Hypnosis: How to Put a Smile on Your Face and Money in Your Pocket

Leonard Susskind — page 81
The Cosmic Landscape: String Theory and the Illusion of Intelligent Design

James D. Tabor — page 77
The Jesus Dynasty: The Hidden History of Jesus, His Royal Family, and the Birth of Christianity

Henry David Thoreau — page 96
Thoreau: A Book of Quotations

Kip Thorne	page	9

> *Black Holes and Time Warps:*
> *Einstein's Outrageous Legacy*

Eckhart Tolle	page	49

> *The Power of Now: A Guide to Spiritual Enlightenment*

Chicago Tribune	page	136

> *Out of the Blue:*
> *The Remarkable Story of the 2003 Chicago Cubs*

Alberto Villoldo	page	125

> *The Four Insights:*
> *Wisdom, Power, and Grace of the Earthkeepers*

Alberto Villoldo	page	35

> *Mending The Past And Healing The Future*
> *with Soul Retrieval*

Jennifer Westwood	page	74

> *Sacred Journeys:*
> *An Illustrated Guide to Pilgrimages Around the World*

Oscar Wilde	page	98

> *The Ballad of Reading Gaol and Other Poems*

J.E. Williams	page	26

> *The Andean Codex: Adventures and Initiations*
> *Among the Peruvian Shamans*

Ernie Zelinski	page	79

> *Real Success Without a Real Job:*
> *There Is No Life Like It!*

CONTENTS - ALPHABETICAL BY TITLE

The 21 Indispensable Qualities of a Leader:
Becoming the Person Others Will Want to Follow
John C. Maxwell   page   69

The 100 Simple Secrets of Happy People:
What Scientists Have Learned and How You Can Use It
David Niven, Ph.D.   page   85

The Active Side of Infinity
Carlos Castaneda   page   30

The Ancient Ones:
Sacred Monuments of the Inka, Maya & Cliffdweller
Hans Li   page 138

The Andean Codex: Adventures and Initiations
Among the Peruvian Shamans
J.E. Williams   page   26

The Ape That Spoke:
Language and the Evolution of the Human Mind
John McCrone   page 130

Art & Physics:
Parallel Visions in Space, Time, and Light
Leonard Shlain   page   67

The Ballad of Reading Gaol and Other Poems
Oscar Wilde   page   98

Beowulf
R. K. Gordon, Trans.   page 104

*Bias: A CBS Insider
Exposes How the Media Distort the News*

Bernard Goldberg   page   1

*Black Holes and Time Warps:
Einstein's Outrageous Legacy*

Kip Thorne   page   9

Careers for New Agers & Other Cosmic Types

Blythe Camenson   page   56

Chicago Then And Now

Elizabeth McNulty   page   106

*The Comedy of Agony:
A Book of Poisonous Contemplations*

Christopher Spranger   page   144

*Common Sense, The Rights of Man and
Other Essential Writings of Thomas Paine*

Thomas Paine   page   116

*The Constitution of the United States
with the Declaration of Independence
and the Articles of Confederation*

R.B. Bernstein, Intro.   page   109

*The Cosmic Landscape:
String Theory and the Illusion of Intelligent Design*

Leonard Susskind   page   81

Creating Money: Keys to Abundance

Sanaya Roman & Duane Packer   page   47

Dada: Art and Anti-Art

Hans Richter   page   140

Geoffrey Ashe	*Dawn Behind the Dawn:* *A Search for the Earthly Paradise*	page	123
Y.D. Sharma	*Delhi and its Neighbourhood*	page	142
Carl Sagan	*The Demon-Haunted World:* *Science as a Candle in the Dark*	page	39
Richard Dawkins	*A Devil's Chaplain:* *Reflections on Hope, Lies, Science, and Love*	page	86
Mona Charen	*Do-Gooders: How Liberals Hurt Those* *They Claim to Help (and the Rest of Us)*	page	134
Sam Harris	*The End of Faith:* *Religion, Terror, and the Future of Reason*	page	128
Idries Shah	*The Englishman's Handbook*	page	83
Aleister Crowley / Hymenaeus Beta X°	*The Equinox, Volume III, Number 10*	page	3
Rhonda Britten	*Fearless Living:* *Live without Excuses and Love without Regret*	page	54
don Miguel Ruiz	*The Four Agreements: A Practical Guide* *to Personal Freedom, a Toltec Wisdom Book*	page	45

The Four Insights:
Wisdom, Power, and Grace of the Earthkeepers
Alberto Villoldo   page 125

Freedom In Exile:
the Autobiography of the Dalai Lama
His Holiness the Dalai Lama   page 13

From Clocks to Chaos: The Rhythms of Life
Leon Glass & Michael C. Mackey   page 121

The Genealogy of Morals
Friedrich Nietzsche   page 102

Germs: Biological Weapons and America's Secret War
Judith Miller, Stephen Engelberg & William Broad   page 154

The God Delusion
Richard Dawkins   page 149

Great Speeches by Native Americans
Bob Blaisdell, Ed.   page 100

Gurdjieff: An Introduction to His Life and Ideas
John Shirley   page 75

Healing and the Mind
Bill Moyers   page 20

Hypnosis: How to Put a Smile on Your Face
and Money in Your Pocket
Shelley Stockwell   page 37

If Democrats Had Any Brains, They'd Be Republicans
Ann Coulter   page 119

The Jesus Dynasty: The Hidden History of Jesus,
His Royal Family, and the Birth of Christianity
James D. Tabor   page   77

Kalacakra Tantra
Geshe Ngawang Dhargyey   page   8

The Law of Attraction:
The Basics of the Teachings of Abraham
Esther & Jerry Hicks   page   57

Legendary Britain: An Illustrated Journey
Bob Stewart & John Matthews   page 152

Letter to a Christian Nation
Sam Harris   page 111

Letters to a Young Contrarian
Christopher Hitchens   page   59

Libertarianism In One Lesson
David Bergland   page   65

Magical Passes: The Practical Wisdom
of the Shamans of Ancient Mexico
Carlos Castaneda   page   32

Mayan Vision Quest:
Mystical Initiation in Mesoamerica
Cynthia MacAdams, Hunbartz Men & Charles Bensinger   page   72

McIlhenny's Gold:
How a Louisiana Family Built the Tabasco Empire
Jeffrey Rothfeder   page 114

*Mending The Past And Healing The Future
with Soul Retrieval*
Alberto Villoldo — page 35

Might is Right: The Survival of the Fittest
Ragnar Redbeard — page 24

*Mind Sights: Original Visual Illusions, Ambiguities,
and Other Anomalies, With a Commentary
on the Play of Mind in Perception and Art*
Roger N. Shepard — page 90

*The Mind's Sky:
Human Intelligence in a Cosmic Context*
Timothy Ferris — page 63

*The Monuments of Mars:
a City On the Edge Of Forever*
Richard C. Hoagland — page 22

Moral Minority: Our Skeptical Founding Fathers
Brooke Allen — page 41

*Mountains of the Middle Kingdom:
Exploring the High Peaks of China and Tibet*
Galen Rowell — page 17

*Myth of Invariance: The Origins of the Gods,
Mathematics and Music from the Rg Veda to Plato*
Ernest G. McClain — page 132

The Nibelungenlied
D.G. Mowatt, Trans. — page 107

*Out of the Blue:
The Remarkable Story of the 2003 Chicago Cubs*
Chicago Tribune — page 136

Parenting Beyond Belief:
On Raising Ethical, Caring Kids Without Religion
Dale McGowan   page   92

The Power of Intention:
Learning to Co-create Your World Your Way
Dr. Wayne W. Dyer   page   52

The Power of Now: A Guide to Spiritual Enlightenment
Eckhart Tolle   page   49

The Practice of Kalachakra
Glenn H. Mullin   page   11

Real Success Without a Real Job:
There Is No Life Like It!
Ernie Zelinski   page   79

Sacred Journeys:
An Illustrated Guide to Pilgrimages Around the World
Jennifer Westwood   page   74

The Secret
Rhonda Byrne   page   43

Secrets Of The Ninja
Ashida Kim   page   147

The Selfish Gene
Richard Dawkins   page   61

Shabono: A Visit to a Remote and Magical World
in the South American Rain Forest
Florinda Donner   page   4

Spirit & Reason: The Vine Deloria, Jr. Reader
Vine Deloria, Jr.   page   51

Thoreau: A Book of Quotations
Henry David Thoreau   page   96

Tibet: The Sacred Realm - Photographs 1880-1950
Lobsang P. Lhalungpa   page   15

*Useful Idiots: How Liberals Got It Wrong
in the Cold War and Still Blame America First*
Mona Charen   page   88

*The Wheel of Time:
The Kalachakra in Context*
Geshe Lhundub Sopa   page   6

*The Wheel of Time: The Shamans of Ancient Mexico,
Their Thoughts About Life, Death and the Universe*
Carlos Castaneda   page   28

Who's Looking Out for You?
Bill O'Reilly   page   70

The Whole Shebang: A State-of-the-Universe(s) Report
Timothy Ferris   page   94

Wisdom and Compassion: The Sacred Art of Tibet
Marylin M. Rhie & Robert A. F. Thurman   page   19

www.ingramcontent.com/pod-product-compliance
Lightning Source LLC
Chambersburg PA
CBHW060517100426
42743CB00009B/1346